Middle Mania Two!

Imaginative Theater Projects
for Middle School Actors

Middle Mania Two!

Imaginative Theater Projects for Middle School Actors

by Maureen Brady Johnson

YOUNG ACTORS SERIES

A Smith and Kraus Book

A Smith and Kraus Book
Published by Smith and Kraus, Inc.
177 Lyme Road, Hanover, NH 03755
www.smithkraus.com

First Edition: July 2003
10 9 8 7 6 5 4 3 2 1

Cover and Text Design by
Julia Hill Gignoux, Freedom Hill Design

Library of Congress Cataloguing-In-Publication Data
Johnson, Maureen Brady.
Middle mania 2: imaginative theater projects for middle school actors /
by Maureen Brady Johnson. —1st ed.
p. cm. — (Young actors series)
ISBN 1-57525-329-1(vol 2)
1. Improvisation (Acting) 2. Acting. 3. Puppet theater. 4. Acting—Study
and teaching (Middle school) I. Title. II. Series.
PN2071.I5 J628 2001
792'.028—dc21
2001054942

To my husband, Mark
My children, Erin, Allison, Juliet, and Sean
My parents, my family, my friends,
my students, and my teachers
who never stopped believing in me.

ACKNOWLEDGMENTS

To all the people at Smith and Kraus for their support

To the administrators and teachers at Lake Ridge Academy for their encouragement

To all of my students for their willingness to try new things

Contents

Foreword

For almost sixty years, as a teacher, administrator, and playwright/director, theater has been an unfailing source of joy and discovery and at the same time a worrisome, nagging, and demanding, albeit cherished, companion. It's a tough road to the emotional and intellectual fireworks of creativity, whether it's the spark of an idea or the work of the art itself.

As the managing director of a professional, not-for-profit theater with a three-million-dollar budget, one has a powerful sense of accomplishment in providing support for an artistic excellence to the life of the community.

But the true arrows of creativity in the theater are shot into the hearts of the artists and teachers. They are the ones who experience the bonding inherent in giving birth to the art of the theater — the playwrights and directors who are one with the audience and the teachers who guide their students through the craft, the art, the demands, the joy of theater and who continue to learn as they teach.

Those of you who read Maureen Brady Johnson's first book, *Middle Mania!* and are now about to read her second, are fortunate indeed. She's a talented theater artist and teacher who possesses an exceptional sensitivity to her students and an ability to inspire creativity in them. She is never at a loss to see potential and take advantage of opportunities for her students. Her sense of community with other teachers has led to her sharing her insights and programs with them.

Many years ago, when I started to teach drama, I followed the timeworn model: encourage students to attend theater productions in the community and then produce plays. Choose the play, cast the play, rehearse until the director, cast, and crews are ready to drop, and then open. A self-imposed guideline was to choose plays that were worth the hard work of memorizing. There is a great value in this approach to work. Students learn dramatic literature, the production process, and creative interpretation. It's good, but it's also necessary for students to become immersed in basic creative instincts and learn where the heart of drama lies. This is the thrust of Maureen Brady Johnson's writing.

An incredible bonus for teachers is the bond that forms between them and students. One of my great joys is that I still hear from students in all walks of life — some who are in their forties and fifties. Much to my delight, they confirm my belief in the value drama plays in education, indeed in life. Maureen Brady Johnson is among those former students, one whom I am fortunate to have as a friend.

Mary Fournier Bill
Retired Managing Director of
The Great Lakes Theatre Company
Playhouse Square
Cleveland, Ohio

Introduction

It's the end of August. Teachers' meetings are in full swing. You've just been informed that you are teaching a drama class to the seventh grade . . . and you don't know where to begin.

The good news is that your school system is realizing how powerful drama can be when taught in middle school.

The bad news is that you have half the seventh grade for one semester and the other half for the second semester . . . during the last period of the day . . . every day. This also happens to be the period of the day when any teacher can pull a student for tutoring, community service projects — and sometimes sports teams have to leave early for games — and on and on.

You've been asked to use this class to put on a play. You have to find a show with fifteen to fifty parts that will give each and every student a chance to shine with a few lines, a great dance number, and really cool costumes. How are you going to do this with half the kids missing half the time?

Sound like a nightmare? It has happened and keeps happening in school systems across the nation. Where can a teacher go for help?

The Internet has all kinds of resources. Google is a great search engine. The Educational Theater Association is located in Cincinnati, Ohio, and offers a wide variety of resources. But maybe you want to talk to a "real" drama teacher or connect with a group of veteran teachers. You are overwhelmed!

STOP. Take a deep breath and catch a case of middle mania.

Middle Mania Two! is based on the theory that you *can* do drama in middle school without relying on the tried-and-true method of producing a play with a hierarchy so deadening to the energy and creativity of the middle school student.

Middle Mania Two! believes that every student is part of the community created when drama happens. It is dedicated to keeping kids safe onstage, building confidence slowly through a wide variety of dramatic opportunities, and strengthening skills while having fun. The projects make natural connections between other disciplines like social studies, music, and language arts.

How do I know this happens? I've taught it and it works! The first book I wrote, *Middle Mania!,* has helped teachers from Texas to Alaska, from Cleveland to Poland. *Middle Mania Two!* explores even more projects that you can use right out of the book or adapt to your particular classroom situation.

I wanted to write a series of books that sit dog-eared on a teacher's desk — books that are easy to use and read like a conversation with an old friend. These projects work for any teacher who wants to use drama in the classroom.

Teaching middle school takes a special kind of courage and creativity. You need all the help you can get! *Middle Mania!* and *Middle Mania Two!* are the places to go to get that help.

Maureen Brady Johnson

The Chapters in a Nutshell

Chapter One: Radio Sound Effects Theater
Grades 6 and 7

Take a short play script; give the students a blank tape and a tape recorder; require them to find twenty-five found sound effects to enhance the reading; make sure that everyone takes a part; throw in a lot of practice time. Voilà! They can produce a vibrant radio drama complete with found sound for a final project. This radio show can be played out for parents and classmates alike.

Chapter Two: Storytelling
Grades 6 and 7

A solid storytelling unit should be a part of every middle school curriculum. By observing great storytellers and then selecting a story for memorization and performance, your students will understand that a strong story is at the heart of every good drama.

Chapter Three: Readers Theater with Hats
Grade 7 and 8

The genre of Readers Theater is a perfect teaching tool for middle school. Its emphasis on vocal and facial expression challenges students to sit still and make the story happen on their faces and in their voices. By adding the special twist with the suggestion of a costume in a well-chosen hat, your students will create characters who come alive onstage.

Chapter Four: Time Machine Speech
Grades 6 and 7

Get your students up on their feet for a speech of introduction. Pair them up and give them the goals for a formal speaking appearance. The challenge to their imagination and creativity is that they must introduce their partner to a specific audience thirty years in the future!

Chapter Five: Garage Sale Monologue
Grade 8

Field trip! Take your students on a quest for a character and support your local charity, too. At a Salvation Army, Goodwill, or church tag sale, your students can search for up to three items to create a character. The monologue that they write from the inspiration of these three items can be performed for a wide variety of audiences. Turn someone else's trash into your treasure as costumes and props for their final performance. Challenge your students' imaginations and playwriting skills.

Chapter Six: Paper Bag Players
Grades 6, 7, and 8

Group your students around one plain paper bag filled with a wide variety of unrelated items and wild costumes. Give them a time limit of days, hours, or minutes to come up with a story rife with vivid characters, conflicting objectives, and a surprise ending. Then refill the bags and switch them around and begin again.

Chapter Seven: "Simple" Play Production
Grade 8

Nothing is ever simple when it comes to producing a play with a group of middle school students. I have talked to many teachers who have been given the task by a department head or an administrator and who just don't know where to begin. This is my story. It will help in your quest for the perfect play production with your middle school students.

CHAPTER ONE

Radio Sound Effects Theater

GRADES SIX AND SEVEN

THE HISTORY BEHIND THE LESSON

NOISE. It comes with the territory if you teach middle school students. They laugh loud. They talk loud. They pick up objects and find every possible way to make noises with them. They even use their bodies to make noise! I began to wonder how I could harness this creative use of sound in a dramatic unit of study.

I have a large collection of *Plays* magazine I inherited from a retiring teacher. In each issue there are about ten plays to perform for all age groups. Sometimes there are classics that have been adapted, sometimes fairy tales, sometimes situational comedies that can be performed in a larger-than-life acting style. I have found them a wonderful resource for middle school drama projects.

When I was searching for projects that would appeal to middle school students' use of sound, I went to these plays to see if I could come up with a new twist. I read through *Dummling and the Golden Goose, The Twelve Dancing Princesses,* and an adaptation of *Alice in Wonderland*. As I read through these plays, I began to realize that I heard them in my head, complete with sound effects. I wondered if my students could take one of these scripts and add their own sound effects, producing a radio play on audiotape for a final project.

This idea especially appealed to me because everyone would have a part in the project, including shy students who could concentrate on their characterization and vocal qualities behind the safety of a recording. I began working on a plan to bring these plays to life in a way that had never been tried before!

BEFORE THE FIRST CLASS

The very first thing you need is a short script. As I mentioned before, *Plays* magazine is a rich resource. The Internet has many sites you can go to find short plays, www.Realistatheatre.com being one of them. I have also had great success with books by Louise Thistle, L. E. McCullough, and Mary Hall Surface. The plays in their books are short and steeped in mythology. I have found a three- to five-minute reading time provides students with enough story line to interest them as they read and reread the script during rehearsal.

You also need to look at the possibilities the play has for enhancement with sound effects. Folktales, fairy tales, and fantasy legends are excellent stories in which to use sound effects. When my students used *Dummling and the Golden Goose,* they used such found sounds as feet walking on a variety of surfaces and many odd noises that expressed the characters getting stuck to the goose as they traveled through town and countryside. Creaking or slamming doors, chains rattling, and ghosts moaning can enhance mysteries. Musical noisemakers such as slide whistles, kazoos, and ratchets can also be used with excellent results. But you must find a script that is ripe with possibilities.

Plays are the best resource because the dialogue provides another opportunity for the students to develop vocal skills. There is an added bonus: Because the students are not acting in front of a large audience on a stage, they are much more willing to experiment with their voices to better represent the characters they are portraying. If a shy student gains confidence in this way, how much more willing will that same student be when he is asked to perform later in the year onstage?

If you find it difficult to locate a play, you can use a story. Again, length is a consideration because the middle school students will grow restless with a very long tale. Greek and Roman mythology and Grimm's fairy tales are all wonderful resources. I love Andrew Lang's series of fairy tale books (*The Blue Fairy Book, The Crimson Fairy Book, The Grey Fairy Book,* and so on); these provide a wealth of folk and fairy tales from around the world. American legends such as Johnny Appleseed, Paul Bunyan, and Casey at the Bat can also be used.

Once you have the scripts chosen, you'll need to locate some technical paraphernalia. This project requires students to work in groups of five to eight people, so you will need a tape recorder and a blank tape for each group. Be sure the tape recorders are able to record outside sound: Many tape recorders today can only record things directly off a radio station or another tape. Usually tape recorders have a microphone that plugs into the body of the recorder, or more commonly, a microphone located on the body of the recorder itself.

I use one tape recorder and tape per group. This allows the students to practice their radio show, play it back, and refine the sound effects that they used, making their production more successful. If you don't have the opportunity to use three or four tape recorders simultaneously, then each group should have their own tape. That way you can avoid the disaster of taping over someone else's radio show!

You are probably asking yourself, "How do I find a quiet place for the students to record their shows?" I use our stage. One group goes backstage behind the curtains to a special taping area. The rest of the class stays in the auditorium itself. They practice quietly or do some homework, while I supervise each group as they read their final piece in the taping area. A quiet place to record is very important, but in a busy school it may be almost impossible to find. Even when we used curtains to muffle the noise, random sounds still made it onto our tape, like a train going by outside or an airplane flying overhead. If you can find a quiet place to record but have trouble keeping the rest of the class quiet, you can enlist the help of another teacher. Perhaps the school librarian would be willing to take the students for a reading session in the library, or you might ask another teacher might take the class for a study hall. Whatever you decide to do, make the taping session as professional as possible so the students will take the taping very seriously.

FOUND SOUND VERSUS PRERECORDED SOUND

This is an issue you need to think about before you introduce the lesson. Some groups will want to use a variety of sounds downloaded from the Internet or sounds from a CD that has previously recorded sound effects. These sounds can provide variety and a realistic feel to the final production. I've always asked my students to use found sounds as opposed to prerecorded sounds. I feel that the search for found sound challenges their creativity and stretches their imaginations. Students learn as they try out different found sounds. For example, a student may bring in a bag to crumple for a specific sound. When it gets taped and played back, it sounds like rain. If that's not the effect that they wanted, then it's back to the drawing board to find another sound that, when taped, is more accurate. One of the groups needed a train whistle; this led them on a quest to the music teacher who happened to have an antique train whistle that they could use. Another group used every possible slurping sound they could make with their voices for the characters in *Dummling* getting stuck to the goose. It is more of a creative challenge to come up with found sound.

If you have students use a combination of found sound and prerecorded sound, it gets tricky technically speaking because then you'd need a CD player or another tape recorder to play the prerecorded sounds. The students would need to be highly organized and have a detailed script with sound cues clearly marked for their final run-through.

The requirements should be spelled out on a detailed handout that you give to your students during the very first class. This handout should also include due dates and specific goals for each class period. Students need to know from the very beginning that they are responsible for achieving a certain amount of work with each class period. This will help them remain on task much more than if they are not given any time limits at all.

GROUPING THE STUDENTS

Arrange the groups that are going to work on the Radio Sound Effects Theater in advance. Some teachers like to let the students choose their own groups. They feel that the students work better when they're with their friends. I like to challenge students to work with classmates outside their circle of close friends. I also like to mix self-starters with students who need a push to get organized and involved. Admittedly, sometimes this approach works and sometimes it doesn't. The dynamics of a group definitely affect the success of the group's project.

Whatever you decide to do, try to work in some incentives that reward those groups who work together well. I give separate grades for day-to-day cooperation, for dividing up the work, and for finishing the work. After awhile, the word gets around that you can't goof off in drama class. Hard work pays off with a performance that the students can be proud of.

You have the plays, the student groupings, the technical equipment, and the place to rehearse and record. You just need to locate one more thing before you begin: a recording of an old radio show. There are plenty of CDs, tapes, and even records out there to use as examples of what it was like to live in the days before TV. I have collected a series of records and tapes with Flash Gordon, Sherlock Holmes, Tarzan of the Apes, and the original Superman. I am sure that you can even download old radio programs from the Internet. I always ask my students who are much more savvy when it comes to downloading things!

Now you are ready to make use of all that noise your students are making!

THE FIRST CLASS

I open by introducing a recording of an old radio show. I prefer Flash Gordon because of all the sound effects used. After listening to a few episodes, we have a discussion about the history of radio shows. We discuss how alive the story we just heard felt because of the sound effects. We talk about how those sound effects might have been made and how even today sound effects are added to movies. This usually leads to a discussion of movies that they have seen in which sound effects were really helpful to the story. I also bring up bad movie soundtracks where the sound detracts from the movie. Most students have seen *A Christmas Story* and can talk about the way radio shows affected the lives of the two little boys in that film.

I then have them listen to a Sherlock Holmes mystery or a Tarzan of the Apes radio program. We then discuss the differences in the shows. I ask questions like:

- Was it easy to follow the story?
- What could be done to make the story clearer?
- How did the sound effects differ between Sherlock Holmes and Flash Gordon? Why do you think they differ?
- What made the story exciting to listen to?
- How did the performers use their voices to create vivid characters?

Then I ask them to describe the physical features of one of the characters. I choose a lesser known character because I want them to use their imaginations. What should come out of this character discussion is to raise the students' awareness of the ability of a performer to create a mental picture of a character through the use of his voice.

Right before class ends, I explain the purpose of the unit and what they will be expected to do. An in-depth explanation is given during the second class.

THE SECOND CLASS

I begin the next class with a thorough discussion of the project. I hand out a sheet that establishes the time line and deadlines. This sheet also contains minigoals for each class period so that students know they are held accountable for completing part of the project each and every class. The groups are assigned, and the plays handed out. I ask if there are any questions and clarify anything that is not understood. The class then breaks into groups and they begin a read-through of the play.

Casting is next. You can handle this in a variety of ways. The teacher can assign the roles before the first read-through, or the kids can decide what they want after the first read-through. I like them to decide on their own because the naturally shy kids take the minor roles. It is a good idea to let the students know that the production needs at least two "techies," who are in charge of the recording of the show and the organization of the sound effects. The group can decide if they are going to have a select group make the sounds or if the entire cast will create the sound effects. By the end of the second class, the groups should have had the first read-through, assigned the cast and tech crew, and perhaps had a second read-through with the correct cast in place.

THE THIRD CLASS

The goal of the third class is to end up with a script that is filled with at least twenty-five sound effects. Each group should read through their play and decide what the sound effects should be and where they think the sound effects should go. The techies should mark the script *in pencil* so that if the group changes its mind, they can erase or make changes without making the script illegible.

There will be plenty of disagreements, so the role of the teacher is to circulate around the room offering advice and settling the bickering. Sometimes the groups will get stuck with only twenty-three sound effects. At this point the teacher can step in with a few ideas. Sometimes a group will disagree so vehemently that a teacher has to help them compromise. Whatever happens during this class period, the groups should end with a script filled with twenty-five sound effects to hand in to the teacher.

Before the end of class let students know that the next two classes will concentrate on rehearsing the sound effects. If someone is bringing in something with which to make sounds, they should make sure that they remember to bring it in or the rehearsal will not go well. The teacher should also monitor the kinds of things that the students are bringing in, especially with today's security precautions. Toy guns brought in for gunshot sounds could present a problem. (Actually, I've done some great gunshot sounds for plays with a plywood clipboard on a flat surface.)

THE FOURTH AND FIFTH CLASSES

The next two or three classes are spent rehearsing, organizing, and redoing the plays. At some point in the rehearsal, the teacher should do a spot check and assess the performance with a grade that has the value of a quiz grade. It keeps the kids on their toes and working hard; it also gives them an idea as to what you are looking for in a final project.

Sometimes the teacher can save the day for a group that is having problems, but the teacher has to resist the inclination to take over the project. Offering suggestions and helping the students reach a compromise is very important at this point.

Acting as a coach helps the students know that you are there to help them with their project — not changing it into something you want it to be.

THE SIXTH AND SEVENTH CLASSES

These classes should be used for recording a dress rehearsal. The students will find that once they start the recording process, all kinds of difficulties will present themselves. The sounds may not sound the same on tape. The group may have to stop the tape and begin again and may record over what was done before. The performers may be too far away from the microphone to be heard clearly. The techies will be exasperated with the performers, and the performers will be upset with the technical difficulties. All these are important lessons for the students. They must adapt and rethink in order to address the problems. This is where some real learning takes place. In all of this, the teacher must be a gentle guide. Reminding them about the positive things that have happened and getting them to have a sense of humor about what happens will not only help their final production, it can be a life lesson!

THE EIGHTH AND NINTH CLASSES

It may take more than these two classes to record the final radio show. This will depend on your students and the progress that they have made, class by class. These classes can also include a playback for the other groups. Time to critique and reflect on the whole experience is necessary. I always use the students' suggestions to improve the project for the following year.

This unit demands a lot from your students on many levels. It is a microcosm of a full-scale production, complete with arguments and compromises. It challenges their creativity and imagination — and it puts all that middle school noisemaking ability to such good use!

COMMUNITY CONNECTIONS

One of the most obvious connections you can make with this unit is to talk to the social studies teacher and find out when they are studying the 1930s and the 1940s. In this period, many famous and historic events were recorded on radio (the burning of the Hindenburg, the War of the Worlds hoax, the Day of Infamy speech by President Roosevelt). You can use your radio shows to reflect the time.

The language arts teacher could collaborate with you on the scriptwriting. Getting another teacher to correct the scripts for writing errors would be fantastic. Conflict, story line, and thematic unity could also be considered in language arts class, and the scripting would be a lot stronger for the final performance. If your language arts teacher does a unit on fairy tales or folktales, the students could study the stories in her class and adapt them in drama.

In the quest for found sound, the music teacher is a fantastic resource. Our music teacher was willing to lend the kids all kinds of strange sound makers. She also took time out to talk about percussive instruments in her class, giving the students a richer background in the original of sound effects.

Another community connection involves the students' grandparents. The generation that grew up without TV is fast disappearing. But many of the students' grandparents remember a time when the radio was the only form of electronic entertainment in the evening. As part of the unit, you could ask the students to get in contact with their grandparents and ask them for firsthand accounts of the time when radio ruled the airwaves. If the grandparents are willing, ask them to come in to give a guest lecture and the students will get a look through a window in time.

As far as another audience for which to play the radio shows, you might want to invite the principal or play these shows for a parents' night. You could also invite a younger audience to your room, dim the lights, and play the radio shows.

One of my colleagues, used a radio show complete with sound effects for a performance night for parents. The students performed the entire show, sound effects and all, onstage. It was like watching an old radio show in a sound studio of the 1930s or 1940s.

TIME LINE FOR RADIO SOUND EFFECTS THEATER

Class One: Listening exercise

Class Two: Project explanation; first read-through; assign cast and techies

Class Three: Insert sound effects into the script

Classes Four and Five: Rehearsing, organizing, refining plays

Classes Six and Seven: First tape-recording of plays with sound effects; refining the sound effects after cast and crew listen to the tape

Classes Eight and Nine: Recording the final Radio Sound Effects Theater

CHAPTER TWO

Storytelling

GRADES SIX AND SEVEN

THE HISTORY BEHIND THE LESSON

I knew that middle school students could tell a good story —
all I had to do was walk down the hall and listen.

"Did you hear what happened to so and so?"

"No."

"Well, she said this to him and then he said this to her."

"No!"

And on and on, as an audience of friends paid absolutely rapt
attention to the speakers.

But these same students would get to class, and I'd ask them
to find a story, memorize it, and perform it for the class, and
I'd get *nothing* — no expression, no energy, no audience hang-
ing on every word in rapt attention — *nothing!*

How could I get these kids to make the leap into storytelling?
How could I get them to realize they were using storytelling every single day of their lives? I began by telling them
my stories.

Our family is always telling stories. Like the story about the
time when our oldest daughter was playing in the backyard

where there was an old wire fence that surrounded the yard. It kept almost everything out, but the neighborhood cats could squeeze through the openings. One afternoon our daughter, Erin, came running up to the backdoor with a piece of matted cat hair in her hand. It belonged to the long-haired cat next door and had been pulled off as the cat had squeezed through the fence. Erin was breathless and excited at her find.

"Look what I found, Mom. A moustache!"

Our family has told that story over and over again. We have a whole repertoire of stories. With four children, we have *a lot* of stories! When we get together as a family, we tell the stories. My students loved hearing my stories. My children, who attended the school where I taught, were not always thrilled that I shared the stories.

But there was a time when this story was told to a much larger audience. When Erin, who found the moustache, was a senior in high school, each senior was expected to give a short speech at the senior luncheon that was part of a graduation celebration at the end of the school year. They talked about where they were attending college and then told a short story about themselves and their hopes and dreams for the future. Erin decided to tell the story about finding the "moustache." But she added a new twist to the story. At the very end she said, "Y'know. The best part of this story is that my parents never told me that it wasn't a moustache. I've always been encouraged to dream, imagine, and create."

Which proves to me that there is more to a story than meets the eye. Stories are the source of truths passed from generation to generation. The tradition of storytelling is strong in our family. I wanted to share this tradition with my middle school students.

BEFORE THE FIRST CLASS

In preparation for this unit, the first thing you need is to locate some videos of good storytellers. Years ago, there was a television show called "Shelley Duvall's Faerie Tale Theater." These stories are enchanting renditions of classic fairy tales. Another series named *Grim Stories* featured a British actor named Rik Mayall. (Mr. Mayall also played Fred in *Drop Dead Fred.*) These stories were as wild as Mr. Mayall's character in the movie! My students loved them. You could also try the Jim Henson series entitled *The Storyteller,* which you can get on VHS tapes at Amazon.com. This is a gorgeous series with John Hurt as the narrator. Another good video is *Sapsorrow, The Luck Child.*

Also try your library. I have found videos that featured storytellers who told folktales from many different countries. These videos are free.

If you are lucky enough to have the money, there are storytellers in every state of the union who will visit your school. The site of the National Storytelling Network online at www.storynet.org lists storytellers, state by state. It is a great resource for teachers and students alike.

Another possibility is to ask the grandparents of your students if they would like to come in and tell their stories to the class. I know that our lower school teachers have grandparents come in to speak about World War II when they study that war in social studies. It is a big hit with the kids and the grandparents alike.

You will also need a number of improvisations that concentrate on storytelling. The directions for some of these simple, yet effective, exercises for making up stories will be included in this chapter. You may already have some favorites, which you will want to use as well. Improvisational storytelling is a lot of fun. It strengthens skills the students will need as they approach their final project for this unit.

You'll need lots of sharp pencils, writing paper, and a good memory for your own childhood and the stories you loved.

THE FIRST CLASS

I begin with a circle, arranging the class so they can hear the stories and feel included. Then I ask the students if they want to hear a story about me when I was a kid. Being the curious students that they are, they say yes and we begin. I am always amazed at how quickly the time for this first class goes by. After telling them a funny story, usually about a time when I was in middle school, I ask them to share their stories. Usually you will have a couple of students who will volunteer eagerly.

Just in case this is a class that is shy or reluctant to share, I do have a backup, which I use if they are not volunteering or which I add after the storytelling exercise. I bring in two or three favorite storybooks from my childhood, and I read aloud *McElligot's Pool, When I Was Six,* or *Half Magic.* For a little bit of time, it's story hour again, and they return to their childhoods and get lost in the stories. When I get tired of reading, I ask the students to read. We all take turns. Before the class is over, I ask them to locate their favorite childhood books and bring them to class next time. Then it will be their time to share.

THE SECOND CLASS

This session begins with an improvisation called Circle Story. We circle up, and I give the students the rules for the improvisation. The first student begins the story with one word, and we go around the circle, slowly at first and then gaining speed. We all add only one word to the story. The story must make sense (though oftentimes it won't during the first few rounds), and it must have a conflict between characters. We go around the circle about three or four times before I call for an ending. Then we begin again going the opposite direction around the circle.

After this improvisation we talk about how we could improve the improvisation the next time we play. This discussion is a good lead in for a discussion about how important a good story is to drama. We talk a bit about bad stories, boring stories, and lifeless stories. Then we talk about good stories, and what makes them great and exciting.

Then we switch to the childhood storybooks they've brought in. Every day we spend five to ten minutes reading and working on these books. In this time the students pick out the favorite part of their book, which they will share with the class later. They also need to summarize the story for the class, so that we understand the part that they will read aloud. If they need to write the summary down, by all means, let them. Stick the summaries inside the books and put the books in a safe place. If you have enough time, one or two students could volunteer to share their stories, or you could share a summary and select from one of your childhood favorites. That way they will know what you are looking for in this assignment.

THE THIRD CLASS

I show one of the videos that I have. I love the Faerie Tale Theatre's version of *The Frog Prince* with Robin Williams. There is also a version of this tale done by Rik Mayall from the series called *Grim Tales*. Mr. Mayall's version is very slurpy and sloppy. The boys especially love it. It also focuses on the storyteller himself and the different voices that he does as he changes roles. Generally libraries have a selection of videos that feature storytellers. Whatever video you use, the students should have a discussion of storytelling immediately after the video.

Usually this discussion leads to making a list of the skills and qualities that good storytellers have and use to tell stories. The teacher can keep the list, or you can assign a class secretary to keep writing down the suggestions.

One good way to make this list is to get some colored chalk or markers and make a huge mind map about storytelling. Then you can leave it on the board as you add to it, or make it on poster board and post it on the bulletin board. The kids love illustrating the points they make. It also looks great as it grows and connects and covers the wall space in the room. Each time you watch a video, finish an improvisation, or listen to a story told by one of the students, add to the mind map.

Don't forget to take ten minutes out for one of the students to share a favorite storybook. The next class will concentrate on writing stories about superheroes.

THE FOURTH CLASS

Begin the fourth class with another storytelling circle. This time we go around the circle adding one complete sentence to the story, instead of just one word. The story must make sense. Your students are aware of this requirement now, and they should be encouraged to try harder to make up a cohesive story.

After the improvisation, if there are any new skills or elements to add to the storytelling mind map, they can do that. This shouldn't take any more than a few minutes.

Next I bring up superheroes. I ask them who their favorites are, what the qualities of a superhero can be, and if they could invent a new superhero, what would that person's powers be. This discussion could go on forever. It is a lot of fun. But the teacher must guide the students to the next task. They are to write a story in which they are the superheroes and they solve some conflict with their unique superpowers.

Caution: Inventing superheroes can be crazy and wild. They need some guidelines, or you'll end up with Puke man or Zit girl. The superhero must be the student, name and all, with a particular superpower that is not gross, vulgar, or crude. The situations must be creative and imaginative, not a replay of what they saw last night on TV or last week at the movies.

If you have any time left over after your discussion about guidelines, they can begin work on their superhero story. The due date should be the next class (which means they would finish it for homework), or you can give them a couple of class periods to work on it. They should refer to the storytelling mind map when writing the story. This superhero story will eventually be told to the rest of the class. They should keep their identity as a superhero secret (except from you, because you need to check it for appropriate subject matter and to see if they are using the storytelling elements). You could even confer with them individually to critique each story while the rest of the class works on their own stories.

How much class time this takes is up to you. I like giving them time during class because then they can see the storytelling mind map and follow the elements that they think are important for a good story.

You may be asking yourself, "Why superheroes?" Well, for a lot of reasons. Students in middle school feel as if they are losing control. They are experiencing changes in every possible way, every single day. When they imagine that they are superheroes, they feel more powerful and in control of things. They are also familiar with many superheroes and the stories of action, conflict, and heroism in which they are involved. In many ways, stories of superheroes are the legends of tomorrow — legends are the stories that people pass down from generation to generation. The superhero stories are a "hook," if you will, to get middle school students involved immediately in the story-making and storytelling experience. Any connections that the teacher makes with the rich oral traditions of ancient cultures and their superheroes will immediately be understood by middle school students because they have created their own legends.

THE FIFTH AND SIXTH CLASSES

These classes should begin with a storytelling warm-up. It is called Fortunately/Unfortunately. The students sit in a circle and one student begins a story.

"Once upon a time, there was a very crabby princess. No one could venture a guess as to why she was so crabby. Everyone in the kingdom tried to stay out of her way."

At this point, the student says the word *fortunately*, and the next student picks up the story along with the change in fortune.

"Fortunately, there was an owl living deep in the woods who heard that the princess was crabby. He was an old friend of this particular princess. She had helped him when he was just a baby owl and he wanted to help her. Unfortunately . . ."

This student ends with the word *unfortunately* . . . and the story changes again. The third student tells his or her part of the tale and adds "fortunately . . ." The students keep alternating until the story is finished. The teacher should keep track of who says which word when because the kids won't remember. This improvisation is a lot of fun and shows how interesting a story can be with a simple twist of fate. Make sure that you add this new bit of information to the storytelling mind map.

After the exercise, the students should spend time refining their superhero stories or meeting with you for a conference. Make sure that you leave time at the end of class for sharing their childhood storybooks. If you do a few each day, you can finish up in a few weeks. This short exercise gives students a chance to practice storytelling and to observe their classmates' presentations and learn from them. They begin to think of themselves as storytellers.

THE SEVENTH, EIGHTH, AND NINTH CLASSES

Each class should begin with an improvisation as a warm-up. The ABCD Fairy Tale exercise is a lot of fun even though it takes up a bit of time. Students pair up, and I give them a sheet of paper. I ask them to list the ABCs along the left-hand side of the paper, skipping two lines between letters; they will have to use both sides of the paper. Then we quickly review the story line of a well-known fairy tale, like Cinderella, concentrating on the main parts of the story. The students then write the Cinderella story using a letter of the alphabet to begin each sentence of the story. The entire story must be written by the time the students get to the last letter of the alphabet. Somewhere around M or N they should be at the middle of the fairy tale.

Give them about five or ten minutes to complete this written improvisation. Then they share their ABCD Fairy Tale with the rest of the class.

The purpose here is to raise their awareness of the concept of beginning, middle, and end. They will really struggle to get the story told within the limitations of the alphabet. Be sure to add this new information about the importance of a beginning, middle, and end to the storytelling mind map.

During these classes, the students also share their superhero stories with the rest of the class. Construct some kind of a set in which the students can tell their tales. It can be as simple as a chair in the midst of a group of beanbag pillows for the audience to sit on. Whatever arrangement is used, it should be cozy. The teacher should give a short list of storytelling qualities that he or she is looking for in this performance.

Each day do about four or five stories. By now, the students should have finished sharing their childhood books, so you don't need to leave time at the end of class for that exercise. I sometimes take a day out to watch another video. This is a welcome break in the superhero tale telling, and the students enjoy the variety and get tips for their own presentations.

A SHORT WORD ABOUT ASSESSMENT

The teacher has several options for assessing the students in this exercise. I find that giving the students feedback as they gain confidence as storytellers is extremely important. Preliminary grades, such as the sharing of their childhood storybooks or their participation in the improvisations, are weighted as much as a quiz.

The major grade for this unit is centered around the superhero tale and its telling. I try to videotape these tales so that students can critique their own performances. The students are usually harder on themselves than I am.

This unit is an immersion in storytelling. The students know that when they walk into the drama class, they can expect to improvise, analyze, create, and tell a series of imaginative stories. They gain observational skills when they watch the videos on storytelling. They develop skills in writing a tale that has a strong conflict and a beginning, middle, and end. The classes blend a wide variety of approaches to storytelling. The students learn that storytelling is a part of their own lives, and they connect to the truths that an oral tradition imparts.

COMMUNITY CONNECTIONS

The very first year that I taught storytelling, I connected with the social studies teacher. In that class, the students were researching a particular country and were responsible for knowing about its culture. I suggested that they find a tale from the country, memorize it, and tell it. The social studies teacher had them research the tradition of oral history in their countries. Some of the students even dressed in the native costume of their countries for their final storytelling experiences. This collaboration gave more depth to the entire unit. It also gave the students a sense of the history of the worldwide storytelling tradition.

Some years we have taken the best storytellers over to our lower school to share their stories about superheroes. The younger students loved the visits, and my students gained the experience of speaking before a very young and sometimes restless audience. A field trip to tell stories at a local elementary school is also a great experience. Sometimes, a tale can be told by two or three storytellers. The drama of the oral tradition comes through loud and strong when the students choose to share this way with a younger audience. They could also read their childhood favorites to these youngsters.

A trip to the local library to find these childhood tales or to find new tales to read and tell to a younger audience is a wonderful idea, too. The middle school students get so excited when they find that the books read to them as children are still on the shelves of the local library!

A connection with grandparents and parents can also be a

rich experience for your students. The students can call their grandparents and talk with them about favorite memories and stories from their past. They can then write out these stories. These can be gathered to create a book that keeps these family stories alive, complete with pictures of these relatives when they were younger.

Since a picture is worth a thousand words, you might want to collaborate with the art teacher and use the pictures of Howard Pyle, N. C. Wyeth, Maxfield Parrish, or Arthur Rackham to inspire some adventure stories. Middle school students could study these artworks and use their imaginations to create their own stories. They could then share the stories inspired by these fantastic examples of illustration. You might even want to use slides of the artwork as a projected backdrop as the students share their stories.

In the musical, *Once on This Island,* lyricist Lynn Ahrens says quite eloquently in the finale,

> For out of what we live
> and we believe
> Our lives become
> the stories that we weave . . .
> This is why we tell the story.

A unit on storytelling is absolutely essential to any drama curriculum. Stories are the very heart of drama.

TIME LINE FOR STORYTELLING

Class One: Sharing our stories

Class Two: Improvisation: Circle Story; children's book summaries

Class Three: Storytelling video; mind map of storytelling

Class Four: Improvisation; introduction of the superhero story

Classes Five and Six: Improvisation; peer conferences on the superhero story

Classes Seven, Eight, and Nine: Superhero Storytelling

CHAPTER THREE

Readers Theater with Hats
GRADES SEVEN AND EIGHT

THE HISTORY BEHIND THE LESSON

I love hats. There's nothing like putting on a hat to get into character. I have a large collection of hats from the forties and the fifties. I also have uniform hats, top hats, and what I call adventuring hats: an Australian bush hat, an African pith helmet, and a 1930s pilot's cap with a chin strap. Most of the time this collection stayed in its storage containers until we did our big musical. That is, until one day one of my students gave me a great idea.

I was teaching a unit on Readers Theater that just wasn't energized enough. One day as I was trying desperately to think of a way to get the kids more engaged in their work, one of the boys arrived early for class and grabbed a top hat I had on a coat tree in my room. Michael was playing the Mad Hatter in one of the middle school Readers Theater productions that was lacking energy. He started to recite his lines, top hat on his head, in a completely crazy voice. His face became animated, his hands went wild with energy. I had found my idea!

I started pulling hats from my wardrobes, and we had an energetic rehearsal with the Mad Hatter leading the way! It was a special kind of irony that the Mad Hatter showed me the key to making my Readers Theater come alive.

A WORD ABOUT READERS THEATER

Readers Theater is an excellent medium to use in middle school, particularly because it is not as complicated as a full-length production, and it gives students a chance to concentrate on their vocal and facial expressions. If you aren't familiar with Readers Theater, there are many books available on the subject. Simply put, it is a dramatic interpretation of a script without the use of any blocking. The students can sit on chairs, risers, or on stools or cubes on different levels. You don't need any additional set pieces unless you want to introduce them. The arrangement of characters on these set pieces is up to the teacher or is sometimes dictated by the script. Lighting can be used for effect, but general lighting can be used to keep it simple. Costuming can be used, but the performers remain seated throughout the show. The voices, faces, and general body tension of the performers are the tools through which the show comes alive.

BEFORE THE FIRST CLASS

You need hats. You don't really need a lot of them, but you need enough for at least one class section.

You can use the same hats for each class section that you teach. For example, if you have a class of twenty-five students, you can group the students into five groups of five, with five collections of five hats. Put the hats into five bags and give them to the next class to use. Using the same hats for each section of drama that you teach saves time and money.

I began to buy hats at secondhand stores for a few dollars. Garage sales, tag sales, and flea markets are great places to find hats at reasonable prices. Parents and grandparents are also a wonderful resource. They will donate hats to the drama department, especially during spring cleaning.

If there is a parent newsletter or e-mail listserve, a note asking for hat donations can increase your collection and provide donors with a nice tax break. Alerting parents early on can help throughout the school year. I had one parent who purchased about ten hats throughout the year because she was always on the lookout for a good hat bargain.

Hats can be purchased from costume houses. Hat catalogs contain top hats, cowboy hats, Canadian Mountie hats, and a wide variety of very unique and interesting hats. If you have a generous budget, there are sources online that sell vintage hats. Auction Web sites, such as eBay, have unique and beautiful hats.

Vintage clothing stores are another resource. They can be pricey, but often once or twice a year they have a sale to get rid of some of their stock. I have wandered into a bag sale where I can fill a brown paper bag with as much as I want for a couple of dollars.

Another resource can be college costume departments. They are constantly weeding out their collections. If you call around to local colleges, you might be able to pick up their discards. Community theaters and local schools can also be a rich resource for unique and unusual hats.

You will also need to locate a script for each group of students. I have used the following sources for short scripts:

- *Plays* magazine: www.playsmag.com
- Realista Theatre: www.realistatheatre.com
- Smith and Kraus Publishers: www.smithkraus.com
- Dramatics Publishing Company: www.dramatics.com

Choose short scripts that take about a half hour to rehearse. That way the students can get through an entire play rehearsal and discuss the changes that they want to make before the class ends. You know your students and you know what length will work best for them. Perhaps you are lucky enough to have a fifty-minute class period with them, and you can give them a lengthier piece. Just adapt the unit to whatever suits your students the best.

Before the first class, you need to locate some exercises for your students to help them develop vocal and facial expression. Having a series of short warm-ups that concentrate on developing these skills is imperative. The students need to have fun with these improvisations, and the teacher needs to help them see the connection between these skill-strengthening exercises and the Readers Theater they are about to begin.

One extremely successful warm-up I use is Walk the Talk. For this exercise, the students need room to walk, so you will need a big space. Move the desks to the side of the classroom, or use the back of the stage. Have the students line up along the wall or the back of the stage.

The teacher stands at the front of the stage or classroom, facing the students. The teacher has a list of descriptive words (adjectives and adverbs) such as: *slowly, quickly, silly, quietly, scared, shy, crazy, timid, sneaky, loud, goofy*, and *angry.*

The teacher whispers a word to the first student in line. The student then walks forward in a way that expresses the word. Then he or she turns to the class — which is still lined up against the wall — and says the word out loud, using his or her voice and face to give meaning to the word. Then the other students imitate the walk to the front of the stage, saying the word exactly as they saw it done by the first student. They then return to their original positions along the wall or stage, and student number two is given a word to walk and talk. The exercise continues until everyone has had a chance. As each person does Walk the Talk, the students usually get sillier and less precise in their imitations. Side-coach them to mimic precisely each time.

When the warm-up is finished, the teacher should connect the exercise directly to the Readers Theater experience. Make specific connections like, "John, I really liked that vocal intonation you used for your word. It could work for the character of the White Rabbit in your Readers Theater. Why don't you try it when you rehearse today?"

The next time you use the warm-up, you might want to let the students think of their own words. Make sure that they use adjectives and adverbs that help them stretch.

A CREATIVE TWIST

You could use the hats as an inspiration for an original script, or you could use a series of connected monologues, a collection of poetry written by the students united by theme, or a recurring character could be used as an imaginative alternative. For example, a group of five students might be given the hats of a policeman, a firefighter, a nurse, a doctor, and a soldier. The students could consider the theme "Heroes of Today," and write a monologue that one of these modern-day heroes would deliver. Working with a language arts teacher would help with perfecting the script.

It's a good idea to group the students before the first class. When grouping the students, you can put self-starters with students who need a push. You might want to cast the Readers Theater with the students you feel best suit the parts. This will lead to an automatic grouping. If one play needs six players then that group is decided as those six. If another play needs eight players then that group is eight, and so on. You might put friends together if you feel that they will work better together, or you might put opposites together if you feel your students need a challenge.

You've got the hats, the scripts, the improvisational exercises, and the groups. Time to try this unit on!

THE FIRST CLASS

Begin the first class with the improvisation, Walk the Talk. After everyone has had a chance to participate, the teacher should lead the class in a discussion about how important it is to use the voice and face in performing.

Pass out the Readers Theater with Hats Assignment Sheet

(see page 79) and explain the goals. I also explain the way in which the students will be assessed. We review the deadlines for the unit. If there is a final performance, we talk about who the audience will be. We also talk about where and when it will be performed. This is very important for your class to know. I have found that springing a "surprise" audience or performance on students can lead to problems. It's best to prepare your students. The goal is to give the students the best possible performance experience, not to create a fearful environment.

If you have time, another improvisation can be used in the last minutes of class, or you can repeat the Walk the Talk improvisation. Sometimes your students will really want to repeat the improvisation, and sometimes they will not.

THE SECOND CLASS

Begin the class with another improvisation exercise that supports vocal and facial expression. Because you will be performing the Readers Theater sitting down, a good improv to try is a classic, The Hitchhiker.

In The Hitchhiker, everyone performing stays seated 90 percent of the time. Set up five chairs, two in front and three behind, so that they resemble a car's seating. The object of this exercise is to adapt the characteristics of the newest person to enter the car. The driver is neutral at the start and picks up a hitchhiker. The hitchhiker enters the car with a trait or quirk that has been chosen by the hitchhiker in advance. It could be something as simple as a continuing hiccup or something as complex as a fear of animals seen out the window. The driver tries to figure out what the quirk is and then imitates the trait; they drive for a while. Then another hitchhiker is picked up and everyone in the car imitates the new trait that the new rider displays. The improvisation continues until the car is filled. Then the teacher picks a new group to play.

A discussion should follow in which the teacher points out how the performers used their faces, voices, and body tensions while performing sitting down. Then the teacher should explain the art form of Readers Theater. Once students understand the exercise, the teacher can announce the groups and pass out the scripts. The groups should have their first read-through before the end of the class.

THE THIRD CLASS

Begin the third class with another improvisation. I would suggest repeating Walk the Talk at this point. It will imprint the process, and students will understand how it is related to their rehearsal and their performance in a way that they could not understand before.

Next, the groups should have another read-through. The teacher can circulate, offering preliminary suggestions about how students can improve their characters. After the groups finish this read-through, call the class together and talk about hats.

Ask the class about hats in general: the history of hats, their use, professionals who wear hats, the kind of protection they provide. You might give a few hats (hats that you are *not* going to use in the performance) to a group of students and ask them to do a quick improvisation using the hats to define their characters. Give them a situation and a basic conflict and let them have a few minutes to get a short skit together. Then have them perform the skit for the class.

After the improvisation, you can discuss how the hats helped define the characters and added to the idea of "getting into character." Depending on your class, you may want to repeat this improvisation, or you can begin the next section of the unit, giving each group the bag of hats they will use in their performance.

Before giving out the hats, it's important for you to make it clear to the class how to treat the hats, especially if you are using vintage pieces. Call it "Hat Etiquette," but make it very clear that you do not want to see hats sailing through the air, being crumpled, or being left around at the end of class. This may seem unnecessary, but I have worked with some of the most responsible middle school kids who suddenly decide to take a vintage 1940s Stetson and make a football out of it!

There will probably not be any time to have another read-through, but the students will be excited to begin their next class with the hats.

THE FOURTH CLASS

A read-through with hats should be the first activity. After a short review on "Hat Etiquette," pass out the hats and begin the rehearsal. The teacher should circulate, take notes, and offer suggestions. The class should try to get through the play two times with the hats. Give the second run-through a grade. This grade should be equivalent to a quiz grade. It is great motivation for the students to stay on task. If the students do not have enough time to rehearse twice, then the teacher should tell them that they will be graded on their progress during the next class.

THE FIFTH AND SIXTH CLASSES

These classes involve a lot of teacher input. The preliminary critique and grade are given to every group. The assessment is based on:

- vocal expression
- facial expression
- energy and vitality of the reading
- characterization
- focus and concentration

This list may look short, but I have found that when you ask the students to concentrate on a few elements and skills, they have more success in the development of those skills. The groups that are not being critiqued by the teacher can be practicing their play, or you can have them watch and critique along with you.

Sometimes the students are the best critics because they pick up things that a teacher might overlook.

At this point in the rehearsal schedule, the students should be very familiar with the script. So familiar, in fact, that they should not need to look at it very often. Script familiarity should be added to the final critique sheet that the teacher uses.

THE SEVENTH CLASS

This class period should be the final rehearsal for each group. The teacher can circulate, encouraging the performers to refine their acting style.

THE EIGHTH, NINTH, AND TENTH CLASSES

You may not need all this class time, or you may need more. It all depends on the progress you have made, how much time you want to give the students to rehearse, and what you expect the final performance to be.

I always videotape the productions. I do this because then the students get a chance to see their performances. Self-critique is very valuable. I am always amazed at students' perception and ability to improve their acting ability when they are given a chance to see themselves on tape.

I also require the other groups to be the audience for the group I am taping. I usually invite another class to be an additional part of the audience. If the students know that they will be performing for a brand-new group of people, they try harder to make their final even more polished and refined.

THE ASSESSMENT OF READERS THEATER WITH HATS

In the Grade Assessment Sheets in the back of this book I have included teacher assessment sheets.

COMMUNITY CONNECTIONS

You can write your own Readers Theater and take it out on tour to nursing homes, grade schools, or libraries. This is particularly effective when you group the hats by theme.

Historical scripts can be found and performed for social studies classes. There are even scripts about grammar, mathematics, and science that could be performed for these classes in elementary schools.

Simple hats could be constructed in art class and then original scripts written and performed. These hats could be fantastical and imaginative, and the scripts futuristic and strange.

The simplicity of Readers Theater and its emphasis on the student's voice and face makes this unit a perfect project to videotape and show on parent curriculum nights. The hats energize the performance and add an extra dimension to the production. There's a saying that says, "The hat makes the man." In this case I say, "The hat helps the student believe that he or she can."

TIME LINE FOR READERS THEATER WITH HATS

Class One: Improvisation and project explanation
Class Two: Improvisation and group read-through of script
Class Three: Improvisation; group read-through and teacher critique; hat improvisation
Class Four: Read-through twice with the hats; second read-through graded by teacher
Classes Five and Six: Rehearsals
Class Seven: Final Dress Rehearsal
Classes Eight, Nine, and Ten: Videotaping final performances

CHAPTER FOUR

Time Machine Speech

GRADES SIX AND SEVEN

THE HISTORY BEHIND THE LESSON

One of the most important classes I've ever taken was a speech class. (Thank you, Sister Donna!) The class taught me so many life lessons it's impossible to list them all. Two of the most important lessons I learned were how to organize my thoughts and how to communicate clearly and effectively. Because I had such a positive experience with my speech class, I was absolutely convinced that I needed a unit on speech for all of my middle school students. I wanted my students to know how to organize and deliver a speech by the time they entered upper school.

I clearly remember the first curriculum night with middle school parents. I reviewed my curriculum for them, and they listened politely. When I came to the reasoning behind why I wanted to teach a unit on speech, parents of sixth, seventh, and eighth grade students smiled and nodded in agreement. Some parents stayed after the presentation just to tell me how much they supported my teaching a unit on speech. With their nod of approval, I incorporated a unit of speech for all grade levels in middle school.

Teaching a unit on speech to middle school students can be challenging. Standing still to deliver a speech can almost be painful for the high-energy middle schooler. Organization can also be a challenge: Look inside any middle school locker, and you'll see how difficult it can be. The search was on to find a way to have fun with speech while teaching these important skills. I found the answer by taking an old-fashioned speech unit and putting a new spin on it.

Introducing a person to a gathering of people is a pretty standard speech, but putting your partner thirty years in the future can add a new dimension to that speech. It can challenge the imagination, tap into a sense of humor, and provide a hook for middle school students to engage them in the study of giving a speech. I named the exercise Time Machine Speech.

BEFORE THE FIRST CLASS

Teaching this unit involves some very simple preparations. Putting together a simple explanation of the project and all the minispeeches that lead up to the final speech helps students understand how they will be assessed and what you expect from them during class time.

For one of the minispeeches, you will need some index cards and a box in which to put them. In the Assignment Sheets is a form that I use when we do this exercise. You can invent your own form or amend the one in the back of the book — whatever works for you.

The Time Machine Speech is very easy to do. You need to pair your students up. They will work with these partners on their speech of introduction. If you have an uneven number of students, you can partner three students together making sure the students know who is introducing whom. The speech itself will concentrate on introducing a partner as he or she will be thirty years in the future. The introduction will include things like the background of the person being introduced, the books he or she has written, honors he or she has acquired, and an anecdote about this person. All these requirements will be explained later in the chapter. As preparation for this unit, a teacher should be able to list for the students the main skills for speech making:

1. Eye contact with the audience as you give the speech.
2. Never read your speech. Rehearse it so thoroughly that you only need a few words on a note card to trigger your memory.
3. Speak clearly and loudly enough for your audience to hear you.
4. Organize your speech so it is easy to follow and so it has a beginning, a middle, and an end.
5. Try to present yourself in a calm, confident way.
6. Make the speech short and to the point. Don't ramble.

You will be introducing a few short speech-making assignments to prepare for the more extensive speech of introduction. These speeches will be coupled with some improvisations and relaxation exercises to get the students prepared mentally for their Time Machine Speech. These speeches will be

1. a simple spontaneous introduction
2. the "Best Time I Ever Had" speech
3. an extemporaneous speech
4. a speech to persuade
5. point/counterpoint

All of these speeches will be graded. The major grade of the quarter, though, will be the Time Machine Speech.

THE FIRST CLASS

You will need to get a CD of classical music and a CD player for the first class. Ask the students to lie down on the stage, or if you teach in a classroom, to put their heads down on their desks. If they are lying on a stage, make sure they have space around them and aren't close enough to disturb each other. Ask them to close their eyes and just relax, letting their minds wander as they listen to the music. Play the music for at least two minutes.

Ask them to sit up and begin a discussion about relaxation. Guide their discussion with such questions as:

1. What happened to your thoughts as you listened to the music?
2. Did you see any pictures in your mind?
3. Did your muscles relax as the music played?
4. What does a relaxed body have to do with being an effective performer?
5. What are some things that cause your body to be tense?
6. What is the thing that most people fear most?

The answer to the last question is speaking in public! The students will probably volunteer such answers as spiders, snakes, dark places, falling, and so on, but the number one fear is the simple act of speaking in front of an audience.

Next, ask your students what they could do to relax their bodies before they get up to speak. Let students come up with a list of things to do to relax and feel confident. Keep this list on hand during this project and refer back to it to reinforce the points that the students themselves have compiled to help with preparing a successful speech.

Explain the unit on speech, including how you will assess the students. Let them know that some of the speeches will be "on the spot," and others you will want them to prepare in advance. By the time the students get to the final Time Machine Speech, they will feel much more confident about speaking in front of an audience.

THE SECOND CLASS

Begin this class with the relaxation exercise that you did for the first class. Choose different music, but keep it classical. After the relaxation exercise, have the students sit up and give them each a number. Ask them to remember that number and to think about three interesting, unique things about themselves.

Tell the class that you are going to introduce yourself to them. You are going to include some factual information, such as your name and where you were born, and also three interesting and unique things about yourself. You are also going to concentrate on staying calm and speaking clearly enough to be heard. Then do exactly that. It should take just about a minute.

Next ask the student with the number one to come up in front of the class and introduce herself to the class. After about the first five speeches, take time out to comment on the speeches, without critiquing any student in particular. The objective now is just to get the students up on their feet. Let the rest of the class finish their speeches, stopping every five speeches or so to offer suggestions or ask general questions. Finish up the class by praising students for their first efforts at speaking. The next class will be more complex and difficult.

THE THIRD CLASS

Begin this class by having students get into their relaxation positions. Wait until the class is completely quiet and do not play any music for one full minute. Do not let the students talk. Then ask the students to sit up and tell you what they heard. They will immediately say, "Nothing." Persist in asking what they heard until they begin to realize that they really did hear "something."

The idea behind this warm-up is to surprise students with the sounds that they *can* hear when listening carefully. I always make the distinction between "hearing" and "listening" at this point. We also talk about:

1. how noise can be a distraction
2. how an audience can have the "noise" of stress in their heads, which distracts them from listening
3. how being a good audience means relaxing and listening
4. how a speaker can tell if an audience is bored and not listening to the speech

Next, read them a two-minute speech that you have written on paper. Make sure that you *read* it from the paper without looking up at them. Then ask them to analyze your performance. The points you want to make are:

1. Being a good listening audience is difficult when the speech is read verbatim.
2. Eye contact is absolutely necessary. It lets audience members know that the speaker is interested in them and wants to communicate something important to them.
3. A successful speech is like talking to a group of friends. It should be natural and relaxed.

Keep track of the suggestions that the class makes about your speech. Add these to the list that you made during the last class. If you have enough time, try taking their suggestions and delivering at least part of the speech the "right" way to show them immediately what you expect them to do when they get up to speak.

THE FOURTH AND FIFTH CLASSES

Ask the students to write a short essay about the best time they ever had. It could be about a special vacation they took, a surprise party, or just a favorite memory they have. The essay should be at least a page in length. If you wish, you could play some of that classical music you used for relaxation as they write these short pieces.

Next, ask the students to read the essays silently to themselves. Then they should circle ten key words from the essay and put them on an index card you give them. Collect all the essays. Then ask them to get up, one at a time, and give a short speech using the ten words as a guide. You will be grading these speeches on how clearly students communicate their stories and on their eye contact with the audience. Tell the students in the audience that *they* will be graded on their ability to listen effectively.

If you stop to critique every two or three speeches, you can make points about what you are seeing and hearing. Depending on the size of your class, you may need to use the fifth class to complete this exercise. The points you want to make are:

1. Trying to keep track of your story and communicate it successfully to your audience is difficult.
2. Practicing a speech with the key words is absolutely necessary for a smooth delivery.
3. Telling an amusing story can capture your audience's attention.

Make sure that if you come up with any other suggestions on successful speech making, you add them to the list you've been compiling.

THE SIXTH CLASS

At the beginning of this class, ask students to write a controversial issue on a piece of paper. These issues can be as wide-ranging as why the school cafeteria doesn't sell a particular item to an important political conflict in the world. Then the students should fold these papers and put them into a box.

Explain to the students that you are going to ask them to choose a sheet of paper and talk about it for one full minute. They must use the full minute. They will protest that they might not know enough to speak for the full minute, but tell them that they must try.

After about five extemporaneous student speeches, stop to talk about the students' efforts. Ask about how they felt just getting up to speak without any preparation. Ask them about how different the speech would have been if they had had time to research the topic. Zero in on how spontaneity gives energy and life to a speech. The points you want to arrive at are:

1. Research for particular types of speeches is absolutely necessary.
2. Spontaneity gives energy and life to a speech.
3. Depending on the controversial nature of the issue and how passionately they feel about the issue, audience members will be actively engaged or completely bored.

A short discussion about these speeches should not take up much time unless you see that your students need the time to understand the points you are trying to make. Everyone in the class should not take an issue out of the box and make a speech at this time. Tell the students that in the days to come, they will all get a chance to speak on a particular issue. Save the box of papers for the next class.

The next speech is the speech to persuade. The students work on this speech by themselves. They will need to invent an object and try to persuade their classmates to buy it. This object should not resemble anything that exists today, and it should have at least five strong selling points. The speech should be written out in essay form, just like the "The Best Time I Ever Had" speech. Using the same process, they should choose ten words to guide their speech, transfer these ten words to a note card, and practice this speech at least five or six times.

During this class period, the students will just get a start on inventing their product. Stress that they must persuade the class to buy their invented product. Therefore they should use positive and persuasive language.

You can assign the essay for homework. The essay should

not be any longer than two pages. Make sure the students know that they will need to bring this essay to the next class.

THE SEVENTH CLASS

During this class, the students should pair up with each other and read their essays for peer critiquing. They should help each other refine their essays, focusing on whether the speech actually persuades them to buy the invention. They can also help each other craft an effective beginning, middle, and end to the speech.

Then have the students chose their ten key words and write them on a note card. The teacher should collect the essays, and then the students should pair up with a new partner and deliver the speech with just the note card to guide them.

The amount of time that you give the students to practice is up to you. I would give them time in class, and then ask them to practice in front of a mirror at home. The speech to persuade is due for the next class.

THE EIGHTH AND NINTH CLASSES

During the eighth class, the students will deliver their speeches to persuade. The teacher should provide each student with a verbal and a written critique. Remember that this is the first formal speech that the students have given. They should be showing a greater awareness of the kinds of things that should be included in a successful speech, but they need to be told what they are doing right as well as what they need to do to improve. The greatest fear that people have is a fear of public speaking. This fear is not going to disappear overnight for your students. Confronting the difficult task of making an effective speech should be done with care and sensitivity. Your students will come back from their colleges and jobs to thank you in years to come if you are understanding and supportive with this exercise.

THE TENTH CLASS

Begin this class with another round of extemporaneous speeches. If you wish to throw a twist into this, perhaps *you* will want to pick out a topic and speak while the students time you!

Another twist you can add to the exercise is to choose two students to take opposite sides of an issue and have a point/counterpoint speech. The speeches should only run for about fifteen minutes of class time.

You are now ready to introduce the Time Machine Speech. You need to explain the project to students and pair them up for their speech of introduction. On page 80 is a guide for what students should do to prepare for this speech. The teacher also builds on all the techniques and skills that the students have been using on the previous speeches that they have delivered.

THE TIME MACHINE SPEECH

For this final project, the students will be introducing their partner to a very specific audience. Explain the following to the students: "The reason for the introduction will be some honor that is being conferred on your partner, but the twist is that you are introducing your partner as they hope to be thirty years in the future. The introduction will include a short history of the life of your partner, a list of awards and honors he or she has received, a list of books that he or she has written, and a short anecdote about him or her. You must address your audience so that the class knows who is bestowing the award and explain why the award is being given."

The students will meet with their partners during this class to establish the persona of the future that their partners wish to be. The students should fill in the information on the assignment sheet. When they have finished filling in the information, they should begin writing the Time Machine Speech of introduction. This essay should be completed for the following class.

THE ELEVENTH AND TWELFTH CLASSES

These classes should be filled with rehearsing the Time Machine Speeches. The rehearsal should follow the same process that the students are familiar with: reading the essay for their partner, writing the ten key words on a note card, and rehearsing several times with only the note card to guide them.

During these classes, the teacher must sometimes run defense. Some students will want to give some unfavorable characteristics to their classmates of the future. The teacher should circulate and make sure that the partners are OK with the way that they are being introduced.

Some of the Time Machine Speeches my students delivered were incredibly creative. We had doctors who cured AIDS, people who solved world hunger, and researchers who eliminated cancer. Some speeches were very humorous and poked fun at a variety of professions. We had a winner of the Garbageman of the Year award as well as Stuntman of the Century. All the students were pleased with these introductions because I had made sure that they were all happy with their portrayals. Some students wanted to actually make the award, the trophy, or the medal. I let them be creative as long as I had the right to refine the trophies if they were not appropriate. Some of my students wanted to give an Academy Award, but I asked them to be more creative than that. I asked all the students to invent the award, not rely on existing awards.

But my students had the most fun with the anecdotes and the books that people had written. The stories they told were quite clever and funny, totally imaginative. The book titles were the most fun. *Garbage Cans I Have Dumped* and *Meals from the Dumpster* were two of those written by the Garbageman of the Year! The students had a lot of fun, but I had to keep circulating to make sure that everyone was in agreement with their future career.

THE THIRTEENTH AND FOURTEENTH CLASSES

During these classes, the Time Machine Speeches are given. The teacher should critique the speeches on the list of elements established by the class — or the teacher can refine the list to just a few elements. Whatever you chose to do, make sure that students know what you are looking for. If the students have made up the list of elements that they consider important, they will work hard to make the final speech the best possible blend of all those elements.

Videotaping the final speech is a consideration if you want your students to critique their own speeches. If you decide to do this, you will need another class to view the tape.

COMMUNITY CONNECTIONS

If you decide to videotape the Time Machine Speeches, then you can edit the tape and show the very best introductions at a parent curriculum night.

I have connected this unit with language arts and social studies teachers. The students were studying great speeches in history, like "The Gettysburg Address" and "I Have a Dream" speeches. When the students worked on their preliminary essays, the language arts or social studies teacher helped correct and refine them. One year, the students wrote original speeches with the theme of "I Have a Dream." The resulting speeches had a polish that wouldn't have been possible with the amount of time allotted to my drama class.

Another connection might be with the art teacher. Students could actually make the award by making a collage or sculpture. This could lead to a display after the speeches are given to show the best examples of the collaborative effort.

A Web page with excerpts of the Time Machine Speeches and photos of the awards could be a collaborative effort with the computer teacher. Your students could use computer class to design and create the Web page. Parents could log on and see what was happening in the drama and computer classes.

Whatever connections you decide to make, the decision to teach a unit of speech is one that the parents will wholeheartedly support. The skills developed during this unit will support your dramatic productions, and as your students go out into the world, they will return to thank you for the speeches that they developed and delivered in middle school drama.

TIME LINE FOR TIME MACHINE SPEECH

Class One: Relaxation exercise; explanation of the project
Class Two: Relaxation exercise; improvised introduction
Class Three: Listening exercise; reading a speech
Classes Four and Five: Minispeech: The Best Time I Ever Had
Class Six: Minispeech: extemporaneous speaking
Class Seven: Peer conferencing and critiquing of their speech to persuade
Classes Eight and Nine: Speech to persuade
Class Ten: Mini-speech: extemporaneous speaking; explanation of Time Machine Speech
Classes Eleven and Twelve: Rehearsing the time machine speech
Classes Thirteen and Fourteen: Final speech and videotaping

CHAPTER FIVE

Garage Sale Monologue
GRADE EIGHT

···

THE HISTORY BEHIND THE LESSON

I love a good treasure hunt. As a drama teacher on a budget, hunting for unusual, exotic costumes and props is exciting and fun. When I find what I want at a bargain price, I feel just like those people on "Antiques Roadshow" who find out that the painting they purchased at a garage sale for a dollar is worth thousands!

Where I live, spring is the time when people clean out their attics and garages. Every week more and more flea markets and garage sales are advertised in the local papers as people try to get rid of excess stuff. Resale shops are filled to the bursting point with spring donations.

One spring as I walked around the stores and yard sales, I began to realize how vividly the things that people choose to possess, and eventually discard, reflect who they are. It occurred to me that if a performer combined several different things (a funky pair of pink glasses, a pair of striped bell-bottom pants, and an oversized pair of boxing gloves), she could come up with an entirely new person — a new character who might have something to say. With this idea, the Garage Sale Monologue was born.

BEFORE THE FIRST CLASS

A field trip to a secondhand store or a rummage sale is the most exciting way to approach this unit. The excitement that a trip like this generates is unbeatable. It is a treasure hunt that your students will really appreciate. The students will return to your classroom energized and ready to create interesting, vibrant characters for their monologues.

Research your area for secondhand or resale stores. Read the local newspapers for advertisements about church rummage sales. Some stores benefit a particular charity like Salvation Army, St. Vincent De Paul, or Goodwill Industries.

You may want to let the store know that you are bringing a group of students to their establishment and what these students are looking for. It alleviates the panicked looks you otherwise get from the managers. You also need to work out a way to pay for the articles. Ask the store if you can run a tally, if you can pay with a check, or even if they can bill the school.

Arranging transportation for a field trip such as this must be done in advance. If you need permission slips, emergency forms, and a way to pay for the pieces that will be purchased, this paperwork must also be done in advance.

You also need to establish some guidelines for the students. It helps to give them a printed handout in which you detail what they will be responsible for in creating the monologue when they get back to drama class. Students should be told that the secondhand pieces they purchase must be worn or used to inspire a complex character with strong objectives. They will write and deliver a monologue as this character.

Decide on an allowance or budget. Make sure students know that they need to stick to it! Decide on the purchase of costume pieces and props. I usually tell them they must find two costume pieces and one prop. If they are inspired by something else, they need to get permission from the teacher for that purchase.

If field trips are not possible for your school, you can still do this project. It involves a bit more work on your part, but it is worth it. You would need to shop for unusual costumes and props. Then assemble your treasures onstage or in your classroom for the class to "shop." Establish an order of choice among the students (oldest to youngest, month of birthday, and so on), or you will have chaos and bickering.

If money is a problem, ask parents and friends to donate clothing and props for this exercise. You will need to start this effort months or a year in advance, and you'll need a place to store the donations, but it can be done. The donations are tax deductible. Of course, you can keep the donations for the drama department or donate them to a church rummage sale after the project is over.

Before the first class, it is helpful to locate examples of monologues on video. Having the students watch professionals delivering monologues helps them realize how they should create their own monologues. I use Whoopie Goldberg's one-woman show. (Note: Make sure you watch this in advance to see if your students are mature enough for this video.) Steve Martin's updated Cyrano monologue in *Roxanne* can be contrasted with the incredible play of Cyrano. The Hamlet monologues are done by a wide range of actors, including Mel Gibson. Watching one-person shows on video can also be helpful. But some of these shows are for very mature audiences: Previewing is a must.

THE FIELD TRIP

On the day of our field trip, the students are very excited and upbeat. I usually give them a pep talk on the bus about behavior, sticking to their budget, and watching the time limitations that we have. They usually enter the store slowly, and as they begin to get into the exercise, they pick up speed. They dash over to me with a million questions. Did I think the hippie beads would go with the forties-style hat? Could they play a character in the future? An alien? An animal? Be prepared for all kinds of questions.

The checkout takes a while, so make sure you allow time for it, especially if the buses need to be back at school for their next run. It's a good idea if you have another adult keeping a list of things that were bought to avoid confusion when you get back to school. Individual bags for each student's purchases are ideal, but sometimes impossible. Having the students keep track of what they bought by writing it down themselves can help, too. Middle school students *will* forget what they purchased. If everything is packed in two or three bags, make sure that you separate it when you get back to school.

THE FIRST CLASS

The energy of the field trip continues in the classroom. Have the students claim their costumes and props, then they should take them and a sheet of paper and pencil to their desks. Students should put their names on the paper, and then they should fill both sides of the paper with their ideas about the kinds of characters they might create. Tell them that they can't write in huge handwriting; normal script will suffice. Give students five to ten minutes to do this, and make sure that they use both sides of the paper. The reason behind this is that even the smallest, most modest idea can sometimes be the key to the monologue. Then collect these papers and put them aside.

Next have the students assemble their costumes and props on a table or on chairs around the room. They should put another piece of paper next to the objects. You should have a pile for each student and a piece of paper next to each pile. Then have students walk around the room and write at least three words that describe the character who would wear the costume or use the objects in each pile. For example, one student's pile might include a pair of plaid pants, an electric pink baseball cap, and a long black wig. Some descriptive words might be *energetic, wild, secretive.* Three more words might be *loud, obnoxious,* and *rich.* At the end of this exercise, each student should have a long list of descriptive words of other people's impressions of the kind of person that would wear the clothes or use the objects the student assembled. This is important because oftentimes the impression given to others is not the impression that the owner of the clothing wants to give.

The teacher should collect the papers, making sure that the students have signed their names on them, and staple these sheets to the others done earlier in class. Now on to class number two.

THE SECOND CLASS

Open this class with a video showing a professional monologue. Don't explain what a monologue is yet. Just show the video. Then, when the video is finished, ask the class what they saw. Guide the discussion so that by the end of it, the class knows the definition of a monologue and at least five of the qualities of a well-written monologue, for example:

1. interesting character in conflict
2. a story that is clear and easy to follow
3. a strong beginning, middle, and end

Then it's time for defining the requirements of the Garage Sale Monologue. Tell the students that you want them to create a character from the stuff that they bought. They are to write a one-minute monologue to be delivered by this character wearing the costume pieces and using the prop. The audience should be keenly aware of what the character wants and the obstacles that are placed in his or her way. At the end of the monologue, the character should have reached some kind of realization as to whether his "want" will be successful. Indicate that a rough draft of a monologue is due in one week.

Show another video featuring a monologue. This time the class should be aware of what a good monologue sounds like. They should be able to identify what the character wants and whether they feel that the character can achieve what they want.

THE THIRD CLASS

Assemble some random costumes and props. These are not the pieces purchased at the secondhand store by the students. Be sure there is one costume or prop per student. Begin the class with an improvisation. Everyone should pick up a costume or prop. Then have the students get into groups of four or five. Begin with one group, with two students onstage, and the other two or three offstage. The two students onstage begin a scene wearing the costumes or using the props. One by one, call the next student into the improvisation. By the end of the improv, all five of the students are onstage and all the costumes and props have been used.

Continue the improvisation until all the groups have had a chance to perform. You might even end the class with an improv in which everyone takes part. If you have class time left over, you can switch the costumes and props around and regroup the students.

Make sure that you have time to discuss and reflect on the improvisation. Ask the following questions:

1. Can the wrong costume (ill-fitting or uncomfortable) affect a performance? How?
2. How does a good costume help with the performance?
3. How did the prop inspire the scene or a particular characterization?
4. How can you apply what you learned today during this

improvisation to the creation of your character and your monologue?

Be sure to remind the class when their monologues are due.

THE FOURTH CLASS

Begin with an improvisation. In this improv, the teacher gives the "who, what, and where" to three students. Tell the students that you will call out "freeze" at some point in the scene, and one of the students will step forward to deliver an improvised monologue expressing exactly what is really on that character's mind at that moment in the scene. Give everyone a chance to do this improv. Then ask students how it felt to deliver a spontaneous monologue. If their character was truly "in the moment," then the monologue would be easier to improvise. Most likely, the students will say that it was really difficult to suddenly break into a spontaneous monologue.

Another improvisation concentrates on the props, using a prop as a symbol of conflict. For example, give one of the students an old lawn-watering device. The student takes the prop and begins a monologue about how the water sprinkler is the reason for an argument between her and her boyfriend. The last time her boyfriend came over, she sprinkled *him*. He is very particular about his hair and he was wearing his favorite shirt. Now, she is going to throw the sprinkler away because he broke up with her this morning.

This exercise is all about giving props the power of symbols. The fact that the prop represents something other than what it really is can lead your students to add some nuances to their own monologues.

THE FIFTH AND SIXTH CLASSES

These classes should concentrate on sharing and refining. The teacher and students alike should be listening to the monologues and giving ideas to each other about characterization and use of costumes and props. Peer conferencing and teacher critiquing are essential to reworking a monologue.

Sometimes the critiquing gets tedious. The teacher should throw in an improvisation at the start of class or at the end of class to keep the energy of the students high.

THE SEVENTH AND EIGHTH CLASSES

These two classes are for videotaping the final performances of the Garage Sale Monologue. After the class has finished taping, everyone should watch and self-critique. You may want to delay the self-critique for a class or two because the students do get bored being the audience for the monologues and then watching a video of the same monologues again. Self-critiquing is very important though, and teachers should be sure to include it in the experience.

COMMUNITY CONNECTIONS

The biggest connection to the community is the field trip, especially if you are helping out a charity by purchasing the clothing and the props.

If you need to save money, you can join forces with the art teacher and make the props to use in the monologue. The portability of the costumes and props make this a show that you could easily take on the road. If parents and grandparents have donated costumes and props, showing the video at a curriculum night will show how you put their donations to good use. My own parents have seen their hats and coats in several of my productions!

The excitement of the treasure hunt can lead to the discovery of a treasure that is intangible. The wealth of a student's imagination unlocked by a few costumes and props is the real treasure here.

TIME LINE FOR GARAGE SALE MONOLOGUE

Field trip to a resale store or rummage sale

Class One: Brainstorming lists about costumes and props

Class Two: Watch videos of professional monologues; discussion of the dramatic form of monologues

Class Three: Costume and prop improvisations

Class Four: Monologue improvisations

Classes Five and Six: Peer conferencing and critiquing of the Garage Sale Monologue

Classes Seven and Eight: Final performance and videotaping of the Garage Sale Monologues

CHAPTER SIX

Paper Bag Players
GRADES SIX, SEVEN, AND EIGHT

THE HISTORY BEHIND THE LESSON

Observing other teachers and directors is inspiring and energizing. I have been very fortunate, working with mentor teachers, observing at the college level, and then adapting ideas, improvisations, and exercises to fit my students. Veteran teacher Sandy Spike used this idea in her middle school English classes. I was lucky enough to watch it in action as a young teacher.

Paper Bag Players is a brilliant idea that encourages spontaneity, creativity, and cooperation. It is economical and portable, and it can be reworked to fit other disciplines. Over the years, I have adapted and modified this idea. I include it here because it can build on the previous lessons in this book and make use of the costumes and props you have purchased for the Readers Theater with Hats and the Garage Sale Monologue. I also include it here as a tribute to all the great teachers and directors that have so generously given of their time and care, inspiring young teachers to teach theater using creativity and imagination.

BEFORE THE FIRST CLASS

Since the name of this exercise is Paper Bag Players, you need to find extremely sturdy bags to hold the costumes and props. You may want to double up the bags.

In the third class, you will break up the class into groups of five to six students. Each group will be given a bag of costumes and props. Put an assortment of costumes and small and large props in the bags. The costumes should range fro m dresses and suit coats to gloves, hats, aprons, eyeglasses, and ties. You should have two to three times the objects as you have students in the group. That is, if there are six students in the group, then you must have twelve to eighteen objects in the bag.

This is where your purchases and donations come in very handy. Reassemble them in a random distribution and put them into these bags. If you still need more objects for the bags, ask the students to bring in something that they don't use anymore. Ask your fellow teachers and go through your own closet!

A WORD ABOUT THE WEIRD

When assembling these bags for the students, you really need to have a few objects that are difficult to identify, such as large pieces of Styrofoam used for packing, odd-shaped wastebaskets, or oversized glasses. When the students get something strange, it challenges them to think in new and creative ways. Things that are broken work well, too: umbrellas that don't work, old coats, and picture frames without pictures will get your students' imaginations going. Just be certain the broken objects aren't dangerous.

I have a collection of fake leopard-skin hats. They are all different styles and from different periods. If I were to include them in one of the bags, I would likely end up with a singing group called the Leopard Sisters. Coupled with weird eyeglasses and plastic purses, these hats would be perfect for a do-wop group from the fifties!

THE FIRST AND SECOND CLASSES

Improvisational exercises help students get into the mind-set necessary for Paper Bag Players. It is helpful for the teacher to review the basic rules for doing improvisation with students before you begin this unit.

I introduce two new improvisations for the first class and two new improvisations for the second class. You may have your own favorites that challenge students to think in new and different ways. The following four improvs are my favorites.

The first improvisation is very simple, involving a list of random objects. I ask students to write down ten objects on a small sheet of paper, and then I collect their lists. Sometimes I have my own master list to use for the first improvisation; and then the second time we do the improv, I ask for their suggestions. The lists might look like this:

1. yellow rubber gloves
2. bicycle pump
3. dying sunflower
4. surgeon's mask
5. old shoe
6. snow shovel
7. licorice stick
8. mirror
9. plastic straw
10. tuba

I choose two students to begin an improvisation. Sometimes I need to help them with a "who, what, and where" to start the improvisation. After they are into the scene, I pick a word from the list and say it out loud. The students in the scene must work the word I just called out seamlessly into the scene.

The key word is *seamlessly*. It takes the students a while to get the hang of this. Sometimes I do the first scene to show them how it works, then they take over. The scene continues, and at random times I call out four or five more words to get woven into the scene. Then we end the scene and begin another one with two different students. We continue until everyone has had a chance to do the exercise.

Then we talk about the difficulty of working a random word or object into a scene. This helps prepare the students' mindsets for when they turn into an acting troupe called the Paper Bag Players — and they must work with a whole series of random objects.

The second improvisation involves the correct and (mostly) incorrect use of one prop. The students line up one behind one another. Two students go into the center of the room and use a prop as it was meant to be used. Let's say the prop is a large cardboard box. The two students pretend that they are unpacking stuff in their new apartment. The scene continues for a few minutes, and then the teacher says "freeze." One performer is tagged to leave, and the first person in line enters the scene and must think of a totally unique and different use for the prop. Let's say that they turn it into a boat and the scene continues with one actor paddling frantically toward another who is drowning. This continues until everyone in the class has had a chance to enter the scene and change it.

The key to this improvisation is to have a few large props that can be used in many different ways. I have seen some very creative scenes done with foam noodles used in swimming pools or even with a simple plastic cup. It doesn't matter what you use as long as the students get proficient at turning something ordinary into something extraordinary.

During the second class, I continue the games with a sit-down-and-talk improvisation. I tell the students that they will be passing around an object and explaining to each other what it *really* is. For example, I take an old computer mouse and tell the class: "I have here a very old plastic thermometer. When you put your finger on a certain part of this plastic thing, it can read the temperature of your body. Of course, it needs to be plugged into another machine, which doesn't exist any more but that is what it is."

The next person takes the computer mouse from me and says, very nicely, "No, Mrs. J. That's not what this is. It is a . . ."

Then they improvise a purpose for the mouse. We continue around the circle until all the students have had a chance to give their versions. When we play this game, I sometimes use an object that defies definition. No one knows what it really is! Then at the end of the round, I explain what it really is (if I know). I have used old bobbins from sewing machines, weird pieces of plastic that held clothing together, and odd pieces of clothing from the turn of the century. It is really fun to do this because it truly stumps the students.

In the last improvisational exercise, we place a prop in the middle of the room or the stage. Two people, one at a time, happen upon it and try to explain what it is and how it ended up there. A third person comes along and "defines" the object, then tells why it is there, picks it up, and leaves the stage. You can extend this improv with three and four people who happen upon the object and a fifth person who "defines" it, picks it up, and leaves the stage. The person who comes along to define it should not, however, be at all correct about the prop. In fact, the crazier the definition the better the improvisation. Then you can switch props and replay the improvisation.

All these games are very important as preparation for your students to enter the world of the Paper Bag Players. They need to look at something and see something else. They need to open their minds to all possibilities. They need to work together as a group of players who rely on each other to follow the cardinal rule of improvisation — don't say no. If they can do this, then they are ready for the Paper Bag Players.

THE THIRD CLASS

Break the class into groups of five or six. Each group receives a bag with at least ten or twelve pieces inside it. These pieces can be props or costumes, but there should be at least two per person in each bag. Each group needs to use every piece in their bag. Each group member needs to use two of the props themselves. With these rules in place, no one can hog all the pieces, and everyone must take part. They have fifteen minutes to sketch out a story with a beginning, middle, and end. There must be a central conflict, and every character must want something. Conflict does not mean violence, and I tell the groups that I want a moratorium on violence as a solution to a conflict. The central conflict must be resolved at the end of the sketch, and the sketch cannot resemble anything I've seen on television or in the movies. Then I let them get started.

When fifteen minutes is up, I let them perform. We critique each sketch according to the guidelines I set down. We also critique it according to the rules of improvisation.

Usually this takes an entire class period. I tell them that eventually they will be graded on their performances. Each group is responsible for their bags and their pieces. All the bags should be filled with the same props and costumes that were used by their group and returned to me at the end of the class. This is a very important preparation for our next class.

THE FOURTH CLASS

I ask the students to get into the same groups that they were in for the last class. I give them a different bag this time. Each group will have another group's props. The challenge of this class is great. Each group must improvise a sketch with the same rules as yesterday — but they will have to work against the preconceived notions that they have from the previous sketches. Their imaginations and creativity are being put to the test, *and* today they are being graded. (Note: I usually equate this grade with a quiz. The students need incentive to be unique and creative, but they are also new at this.)

Fifteen or twenty minutes later, the sketches are ready to be performed, critiqued, and graded. This usually takes up all the rest of the class time. Make sure that all the props are returned to the bags. This will be important for the next class.

THE FIFTH CLASS

In this class, one group is featured. They will take the stage and be given a paper bag. The scene begins without any preparation. When the teacher says "now," someone from the group reaches inside the bag, pulls out a prop, and works it seamlessly into the scene. They must play the scene out until the bag is empty.

The bags can be lightened for this exercise. Doing an improv sketch using ten to twelve objects is very difficult even for professional improvisationalists. You can begin with five objects and then add more as the students become more proficient at the exercise.

Each group should have a chance to try this variation. I usually have a video to show for part of this class of one of the many improvisational shows on television today. I find that once the students realize how difficult it is to do improv, they really appreciate shows like "Whose Line Is It Anyway?"

THE SIXTH CLASS

This is the last variation to use before the final graded sketch. The bags need to be redone at this point. They must contain about as many items as there are students in the group. Each student must use one object this time — but they must not use it as it was meant to be used. The students must create an improvisational sketch using an object apiece, but in a way that it was never meant to be used.

Fifteen minutes later, the groups perform the sketches, and the class discusses, critiques, and grades the sketch. Part of the grade reflects how the objects are used incorrectly and how creative the group members have been in this effort.

Then we usually have time to watch a bit more of the video on improvisation. Before they begin to watch, I tell them that the next time we get together as a class, they will be working on their final sketch for their final grade on this unit.

THE SEVENTH CLASS

The bags should be refilled with two objects per student per group. There will be some objects that will remain in the same bag, but most should be mixed up. This is the time to include some of those weird objects that I was talking about earlier. These strange and unusual objects will definitely challenge your students and their improvisational abilities.

You might even want to throw them a bigger curve, depending on how well they have done with the improvisations. Once their sketch is started, you can say "freeze," and introduce another prop into the sketch. Or you can say "freeze," and take a prop away replacing it with something else. Or you can say "freeze," and tell the students to use a particular prop as something totally different.

Whatever you decide to do, all these curves that you throw at them are based on the improvisations they have done before. They should be able to adapt and incorporate into the sketch whatever you throw at them if they have learned anything about improvisation at all.

THE EIGHTH CLASS

Have some fun with the last class. Give out awards for the successful Paper Bag Players, which would be everyone in class. You could invent three or four different categories for the three or four different groups in your class. Give them awards like "The Group Most Likely to Use a Dramatic Pause" or "The Group that Got the Most Meaning Out of a Paper Cup" or "The Group that Got the Most Laughter." The Paper Bag Players never take themselves too seriously!

COMMUNITY CONNECTIONS

We have used the Paper Bag Players for our all-school community days. In fact, one time it saved our student council's

School Olympics. It was raining heavily outside, and they had planned outdoor activities. I ran around throwing objects and costumes in paper bags, and each team did a comedy sketch. By the time we were finished, the sun was out and we had laughed ourselves right through the thunder and lightning!

The objects in the bags can be linked thematically. You could do Paper Bag Players with historical objects, science paraphernalia, even food groups for health or nutrition classes. The students could make objects in art class and use them in the bags. Be sure they make durable things, though.

The real community connection is the one that the students make with each other. In any improvisational troupe, the members rely on each other completely when playing in a sketch. Trust between the players is imperative. The Paper Bag Players build trust between middle school students. I can't think of a better community connection.

TIME LINE FOR PAPER BAG PLAYERS

Classes One and Two: Improvisational exercises
Class Three: The First Paper Bag Sketch
Class Four: The Second Paper Bag Sketch
Class Five: Single group sketch and video of improvisational comedians
Class Six: Twist on the sketch and video
Class Seven: Final performance of Paper Bag Players
Class Eight: Awards ceremony

CHAPTER SEVEN

"Simple" Play Production

GRADE EIGHT

THE HISTORY BEHIND THE LESSON

Directing a middle school play or musical can be the most exasperating, exhausting, exciting, exhilarating event in your life. It is very different than directing high school or college theater. Middle school students are a different breed — and the teachers who work with them understand that they require a different approach.

Many excellent books exist on how to direct a play. There are courses that you can take that give you hands-on training. Even with all these resources, I still get e-mail from teachers all around the country asking for help. Many teachers are told during the summer months that they will be directing a show during the following school year. Some of these teachers have never directed a play before.

The purpose of the *Middle Mania!* books is to show teachers that there are alternatives to directing a play. A middle school drama program can and should be sensitive to the unique makeup of a middle school student. I really believe that a middle school drama teacher does the most good when creating a curriculum that is based on building a community where every child feels safe onstage. Play production is not the only way to build community.

That said, I can't ignore the many middle school teachers who ask for help directing a middle school play. I have gotten so many e-mails with questions about directing a play or musical, I decided to include a chapter to relate my experiences directing a production in middle school.

I've also developed an assessment sheet for dramatic productions (see page 98). It zeroes in on skill development in both the process and the product of play production for middle school students. It will help immensely if you are required to give your students grades for their performances. Copy it. Adapt it. Use it.

BEING ASKED TO DIRECT A PLAY

Being asked to direct a play is definitely a "good news, bad news" situation. The good news is that your school and administration must realize the value of drama in the formation of our youngsters' lives. Many teachers still struggle just to get drama into the curriculum. Middle schools need to teach drama. The impact it has on middle school students is unbelievable. Nothing else can and does change young people's lives like drama. Those of us in theater believe this so deeply we are willing to leap into the unknown and direct a play.

The bad news is that very few people realize the number of hours it takes to prepare and produce a play. As well, middle school students are a paradox. One minute they are high energy and you need to focus that energy into a rehearsal, and the next minute they are "too cool" to rehearse, so you have to work hard on motivation. It's not unlike riding a roller coaster . . . for hours at a time!

I have tried to distill the lessons I've learned into a few practical points. I will relate real life experiences to support these points. It works for me. I hope it works for you.

KEEP IT SIMPLE

This doesn't necessarily refer to the size of the production you choose to do. It is more of a mind-set. Whatever you do, whether it is choosing a script, dealing with irate parents who think their children deserved the lead, or setting up a rehearsal schedule, break it down to its simplest parts and deal with it. I know that this is a very difficult thing to do. But it will decrease the level of stress and increase the amount of energy you can devote to a wonderful production.

From the very beginning, my students wanted to do a play — a real play. I decided to take two semesters of classroom time with the eighth grade and do two plays. I had two sections of eighth grade with eighteen students in each class, and everyone would have a part in the production. We met twice a week for forty-five minutes and used the semester to rehearse the show.

I chose two full-length plays, and they were complex, full-length plays. I did not have any help with sets or costumes. I was on my own. I did not "keep it simple." It was a beginner's mistake — a big mistake.

Even though I survived the performances, I decided to search for plays that were not as complex as the ones I tried to do my first year. I found a rich resource in *Plays* magazine. As long as I was going to be doing a play per class, I needed to find a show that could be entirely rehearsed in the forty-five minutes of class, and it needed to have a simple set, simple costumes, and simple technical requirements. The shows would run for about forty minutes each, and an evening of performance would not run three and a half hours, but a simple hour and a half. I learned to keep it simple and to keep it short. The quality of the productions rose because we had more rehearsal time, and parents appreciated an evening of theater that didn't go past the bedtimes of their younger children.

"Keeping it simple" applies to everything from organizing the rehearsal schedule, giving blocking and notes on characterization to dealing with your production staff, parents, and administration. Try mightily to understand what the subtext is when listening to a parent complain or an administrator ask questions. The more I tried to do this, the better I got at problem solving. There is always stress and disagreement when you get creative people together to work on a project. But there seemed to be less when I tried to keep it simple.

FIND OUT WHAT "THEY" WANT

When drama comes to middle school, it is usually accompanied by a "they." You'll hear it all the time. If you can find out what "they" want, life will be so much easier. It is not all that easy because most of the time "they" don't know what "they" want.

If you do a nice little play, "they" wanted a huge extravaganza musical.

If you rehearse after school, "they" can't make it.

If you need to schedule the performance space, "they" need it at exactly the same time because the carpet needs to be cleaned.

You may never find out everything that "they" want or need, but if you try to understand and clarify what is expected of you from the start, it makes life a lot easier. This leads right into my next point.

COMMUNICATE OFTEN AND CLEARLY

With e-mail and listserves, you would think that communication would get easier, but it is just as complex as ever because tone of voice cannot be "heard" over e-mail and sometimes a director comes off as a general barking orders to a willing, yet puzzled, staff. Face-to-face meetings with production staff, parent helpers, and administrators can make a big difference. I am not an advocate of more meetings, but I think a few organized, well-run meetings can go a long way to preventing problems.

When I was a young teacher, I would send out the rehearsal schedule without checking with students and parents beforehand. I ran into a lot of problems that didn't need to exist. I talked to a veteran director and borrowed a permission slip form that had to be signed by the student *and* the parent. This handout included a rehearsal schedule with days and times listed on it that the parents could hang up on their refrigerators or copy in their day planners. It also had a space to list possible student conflicts with the rehearsal. This made me aware of the karate lessons on Wednesday or the horseback-riding lessons on Thursday. Sometimes it meant that I could not cast a student in a lead, but at least I knew about the conflict before I considered someone who, ultimately, could only be at rehearsal for a quarter of the time! This form had to be read and signed by both the student and the parent before the student could try out. From the time I started to use this form, I have had fewer headaches with scheduling.

I usually have one or two preproduction meetings with the staff and a postproduction meeting to talk about what we would do differently next time. This sets up relationships right from the start. A director needs open and honest relationships with the staff. You are all there for the same reason — for the students and their ultimate success at producing a play. Making sure that the meeting is scheduled at a time when everyone can come and can stay until all issues are discussed is essential. Preproduction meetings should take place at least a month or two before tryouts. Postproduction meetings should be scheduled a week or two after the final performance — that is when many problems are still fresh in the minds of your staff. Changes can be made for the following year to avoid any mistakes that were made.

Administrators and department heads need to be kept informed of the progress of your rehearsals. Most principals don't like surprises when it comes to a production that involves parents and the public. Invite administrators to rehearsals and drop them an e-mail to let them know how things are progressing.

Some administrators ask to read the script in advance, and others let the director make the decision about the choice of play. I have always been able to choose the shows I want to do — the ones I feel fit the student talent that I have. The key here is to be sure that you know what the administration wants from the very first time they ask you to do a show. Ask a lot of questions. *Communicate often and clearly* about the choices that you make.

Communicating with parents sets up the roles you want *them* to play for every production you will do in the future. I know some directors who only want parents in the audience on opening night, cheering their students on. I know other directors who could not do the elaborate shows that they do without the help of the PTA Drama Booster Club. I have been blessed with incredibly helpful parent volunteers. But I know a director who had a phone call at 2:00 AM from an irate parent who wanted to discuss the director's casting choices. This same director rewrote a script for the daughter of this irate parent, giving the youngster a larger part. Unless you want to be rewriting every play you do, I would suggest that you *communicate clearly* to the parents that you will cast the show as you see fit. If they are not satisfied with your decisions, then their child should not participate.

ASK FOR HELP

Theater is a collaborative art form. Creating a community of the middle school cast members is not the only job a director has. Your staff is a community created to help the students put on the best production possible. The community of adult collaborators and the attitude that they have toward each other will have a direct effect on the students and their attitude toward the production.

If you are the only person responsible for the middle school play then you need to *ask for help*. I cannot say this too strongly: *ask for help*. There is no way that you can mount a major production without help with the set, the music, the costumes, the makeup, the lighting, and the sound. I found this out the hard way. I tried to do everything myself. I nearly had a major breakdown. Doing everything just doesn't work. The productions I did with a staff to help me were so much better than the ones I did by myself. The experience for the students was a much richer one because they were dealing with a group of calm adults rather than with one harried woman on the verge of a breakdown.

The tone you set as a director from the first preproduction meeting to the last bit of clean-up is very important. Middle school students are highly observant and sensitive, and they will notice very quickly if the staff does not get along and support each other. This tone will seep into the play, show up in rehearsals, and affect the final production.

Define the roles of your staff. *Communicate often and clearly* with them. Never argue in front of the kids. Support each other in public and talk about disagreements in private. Sounds like the advice one gets for a good marriage! But I have seen disastrous things happen when middle school students see a director arguing with a choreographer in a hallway, or when the adults in charge of tech raised their voices — and it wasn't to check the levels of sound in the auditorium.

If the chemistry is bad between the adults in charge, then you clearly have to address the issue. Agreeing to disagree in private can happen, but a professional, supportive attitude in front of the students is imperative. They will model the behavior that they see — and this behavior can make or break a successful production.

GET ORGANIZED

Advanced preparation is essential to *getting organized*. Choosing a play, assembling the staff, and setting up a rehearsal schedule complete with realistic deadlines has to happen months in advance.

Start reading plays during the summer. Keep a shelf on a bookcase for the ones that you want to direct. I have copies of plays that are so funny and clever and well written sitting on my shelves that I have never directed. I know that someday I will have the perfect cast for that production.

Develop a network of directors. Every year I ask drama teachers at other schools what plays they have read, and every year I expand my knowledge of plays and musicals. Talking to someone who has directed a show is a lot more helpful than those descriptions in drama catalogues.

Networking can happen on a professional level with the educational theater organizations. Attending conferences, logging on to their Web sites, and posting notices on their bulletin boards can lead to great play discoveries and friendships that span the country. There is a wealth of ideas out there, but you have to give yourself enough time to discover the gems.

For middle school, I have found *Plays* magazine very helpful. They have had many plays that met my list of requirements:

1. large casts with adaptable parts
2. strong story lines
3. thirty- to forty-minute running times
4. simple technical requirements
5. imaginative, creative parts for students
6. no royalties

When looking for plays, the Internet is a fantastic resource. I just got an e-mail from a friend who shared with me a new drama Web site: www.dramaticpublishing.com. This site has a special feature: You can enter the type of play, the cast numbers, and the breakdown according to gender, and a whole list of plays will pop up.

Original, student-written plays are also a source of some of the most moving productions that I have ever done. But you must begin months in advance. Your cast and staff will not appreciate your doing rewrites at the last minute.

TRYOUTS

You are getting organized. The play is chosen. The staff is assembled. Now is the time to figure out how to run tryouts. For a play, you usually have the director running a series of tryouts for two or three days, with callbacks on an additional two days. The director can have the kids read through a few choice scenes from the show or have the kids show up with a prepared monologue. I usually have the first round of students do monologues. Only the callbacks read scenes from the play. A form is due at the time of tryouts. This form is signed by the parents and the students, and it makes them aware of the rehearsal schedule and the commitment that they are making to the production.

For musicals, you may need the same amount of time for tryouts but with added personnel. The musical director will want to hear the kids sing, and the choreographer will want to see how they move. Running the tryouts with the students singing first, then reading, and then dancing works well for most tryout situations. Sometimes the singing and reading will take place on one day, and because the kids have to change into dancing clothes, the choreographer will have a separate day of tryouts.

Whatever your staff decides to do, don't have endless tryouts and callbacks. It just wears the students down. All the energy and excitement from trying out gets dissipated real fast with a tryout schedule that lasts for a month! Callbacks should only be for students that are being considered for a major role. Don't get a student's hopes up by calling her back if she is not being considered strongly for a role. On the other hand, make sure that you leave some options open for casting a role; don't cut the list of callbacks too short.

We always post tryouts on a Friday at the end of the school day, so the kids have the weekend to grouse about it. This seems to work well. The students come back to school on Monday ready to work on the show. If someone is dissatisfied and drops the show, then the staff always has a backup student in mind to take the role, and we all move to the first read-through.

COUNT BACKWARD

When making a play rehearsal schedule, *count backward*. Start with the final performance, then the dress rehearsal, then the run-through of act II, then the run-through of act I . . . all the way back to your first day of tryouts. The general rule of thumb is: Three weeks for a play, two months for a musical. I have worked with directors who said that you shouldn't work any longer than a month on a musical and others who have taken three months. The best rule of thumb is: Know your students. When working out a rehearsal schedule, a director must know the kids and how many other things they are committed to outside school. Soccer, gymnastics, horseback-riding lessons, and piano lessons were in place long before you even picked a play.

If you need to rehearse during the school day because of schedule conflicts, you need to negotiate that time in advance. It is also wise, if you are doing a play for the first time, to let your colleagues know that you may need time the week before performance to rehearse if you feel the kids aren't ready. It is wiser to schedule that time from the start because you *will* need it. Knowing your faculty and how committed they are to this experience is also important. Pulling students out of class during crunch week can create all kinds of bad feelings and put the students right in the middle of a terrible situation. The more you can troubleshoot these problems in advance, the better it will go.

SET REALISTIC DEADLINES

Knowing when to set deadlines for line and song memorization, costuming and props, lights, set construction, and sound comes with experience. Sticking to the deadlines is almost impossible because something always comes up that delays the work. The paint doesn't come in, so the set pieces won't be ready. The gels for the lights were not ordered, so the crew will need to focus lights the week before a production. Your lead has laryngitis and won't be at rehearsal today. Working with an adaptable staff is the key to your sanity. Being highly adaptable as a director is essential.

The one deadline that can almost be set in stone is line and song memorization. I require that everything be memorized two weeks before the performance date. Some directors require more time, some less. That's why you need to know your students and your staff. There is nothing so painful as watching a youngster onstage struggling to remember their lines during a dress rehearsal. You need to give them the advantage of having the lines memorized far in advance to feel confident onstage. That involves choosing a deadline and taking the scripts away from them at least two weeks in advance.

Costumes and props need to be assembled weeks in advance, too. If a costume is ill-fitting, then you need time to get it altered. If there are complex props to work with, the performers need to work with them consistently over a two-week period. The confidence that a student has onstage depends on using the prop over a period of time. Students also need to take responsibility for their costumes and props. Returning them to a prop table or a costume rack is part of the learning experience.

THE BEST EXPERIENCE I'VE EVER HAD WITH A MIDDLE SCHOOL PLAY

I had three sections of eighth grade drama that year — which meant I would not be directing two plays, but three. That summer I found three plays that fit my requirements: *Camel-Lot, Panic in the Palace,* and *Rhubarb.* I found two of them in *Plays* magazine and one in a very old book of plays that the librarian had given to me. I was determined to *keep it simple,* with one set, a throne room, and changing tapestries to show the audience that a new play was being performed.

I set up a meeting with the head of our school and explained what I wanted to do with the eighth grade play that year. I wanted every eighth grade student to be onstage, even if it was only with a minor walk-on type of role. He said that he thought

I had some great ideas and that if I needed any help I should let him know.

I called a friend who had volunteered to do costumes and *asked for help*. She constructed the most beautiful, sturdy medieval costumes that we still use to this day. The set was so simple that it turned out to be a plus because the elegant costumes really stood out. My husband helped, as he did every year, to do the lights and the sound. Some of the eighth graders volunteered for stage crew. They were the kids who only had walkons, but they were eager to do crew and help out backstage, too. Another teacher offered to do the program, and a mom said that she would get some people together to feed the kids the night of the performance and also do refreshments. I had my staff — and they knew what to do.

I cast the play within each class and the rehearsals went forward. I was lucky enough to have class time to rehearse. I *counted backward* from the date of performance on December 8 and *set up the deadlines* for line memorization two weeks before the final dress rehearsal. I tried to *communicate often and clearly* with the students, staff, and parent volunteers. Phone calls, quick meetings, and notes back and forth kept things going. I worked out an afternoon rehearsal with the eighth grade teachers so that the kids could have their dress rehearsals. I tried to keep in touch with the secretary, who scheduled the auditorium, and the maintenance crew, who needed to clean, to make sure that I had reserved the space at the right time. I really tried to *be organized*.

The night of the performance came, and there was the distinct threat of a snowstorm. I was certain that it would hit and we would have to cancel and reschedule. I really tried to be adaptable, but I was a nervous wreck. The students got into their costumes, but someone was missing. My husband and our children had not arrived. He was my tech director and he was very late. Curtain was at 8:00 PM and he walked in at 7:50. The car had broken down about a twenty-minute walk from school, and he had to walk with the kids to the auditorium.

He stepped in and brought the houselights down, and the plays went off without a hitch. The snowstorm hit the next day, and the car's breakdown was covered by the extended warranty.

Those eighth graders are in college now. They still recall the fun they had doing those plays. They tell stories of things I didn't know were happening backstage — like props being thrown around and spontaneous, silent sword fights broken up by the adult stage manager. I have pictures that capture the moments, and when I look at those photos, the mature college students become sweet, awkward eighth graders again.

This is the reason I teach drama — the students. The community that they create when putting a play together is the real reason to do a play — to put aside the labels of "lead" and "crew" and to create a world together and to help each other out onstage no matter what role you play in the production of the play. It is what's important onstage. It is what's important in life.

Assignment Sheets

RADIO SOUND EFFECTS THEATER ASSIGNMENT

Name _____

Objectives
- To create a dynamic, creative radio program from the play script given to your group
- To add twenty-five sound effects that enhance the story

FIRST CLASS: Read through the script.

SECOND CLASS: Assign parts and choose two techies. Decide the roles and jobs for performers and techies. Have a read-through with the correct cast members.

THIRD CLASS: Read through the script. Decide which sounds will be used and where they will be heard in the script. Remember that twenty-five different sounds must be used.

FOURTH AND FIFTH CLASSES: Rehearsals. Group receives their first grade from the teacher on clarity and effective sound effects.

SIXTH AND SEVENTH CLASSES: Tape recording with sound effects. Replay and listen to the tape. Refine for final taping.

EIGHTH AND NINTH CLASSES: Record the final show.

READERS THEATER WITH HATS ASSIGNMENT

Name _____

Objective
   To produce an energetic, focused Readers Theater production using hats to help strengthen your characterization.

FIRST CLASS: Project explanation.

SECOND CLASS: First read-through of the script.

THIRD CLASS: Second read-through with teacher's critique.

FOURTH CLASS: Read through twice with the hats; second read-through is graded by the teacher.

FIFTH AND SIXTH CLASS: Rehearsals.
   Pay special attention to:
      1. Vocal expression
      2. Facial expression
      3. Energy and vitality of the reading
      4. Characterization
      5. Focus and concentration

SEVENTH CLASS: Final dress rehearsal.

EIGHTH, NINTH, AND TENTH CLASSES: Videotaping of final performance.

TIME MACHINE SPEECH

Introduction of your partner thirty years in the future.

1. What honor is your partner receiving?

2. What group is giving this honor?

3. What has your partner done to distinguish himself or herself in this field? List books written, medals won, experiences, education, and background that would lead to this honor.

4. Write a short imaginary story that tells a bit about your partner in relationship to this honor. Incorporate this short story at the beginning of your speech of introduction. It should be humorous and put your audience at ease.

5. Make sure that you can pronounce your partner's name and job description correctly. Nothing is so embarrassing as making a wonderful speech of introduction and ending with a mispronounced name!

6. Write out your introduction in essay form. Remember: You will only be allowed to take a note card with ten words on it up to the podium when you give your final speech of introduction.

   A. Beginning:

   B. Middle:

   C. End/Closing:

7. Rehearse your speech many times and have your partner give you comments on how to improve. The more you practice it, the easier it will be to use the ten words to trigger your memory. Do *not* memorize the speech. It will sound artificial and stilted. Eye contact, enunciation, and projection should be skills that you work on with each rehearsal.

GARAGE SALE MONOLOGUE
INFORMATION SHEET

(To be handed to the teacher before you perform your final)

Name _____

List the three pieces that you chose to work with.

1. _____

2. _____

3. _____

Character's name _____

What does the character want?

_____

_____

_____

_____

_____

What obstacles must the character overcome to get what he
or she wants?

_____

_____

_____

_____

_____

Written monologue (one minute long)

_____

_____

_____

_____

_____

_____

_____

_____

_____

_____

_____

_____

_____

_____

_____

_____

_____

_____

_____

_____

_____

_____

_____

MIDDLE SCHOOL GARAGE SALE MONOLOGUE
STUDENT ASSIGNMENT AND WORKSHEET

Name _____

List the three costumes/props used to create the character.

1. _____

2. _____

3. _____

List at least five character traits that you want to portray.

1. _____

2. _____

3. _____

4. _____

5. _____

Write up a short history of your character's life. (What does he or she *want*? What conflicts and obstacles has he or she run into?)

_____

_____

_____

_____

_____

_____

_____

_____

_____

_____

_____

After writing the monologue, deliver it to three of your class-mates, one at a time, and write their suggestions down here. They can give you suggestions on your delivery, or the text of the monologue and how clearly it is written.

First Peer Conference:

Second Peer Conference:

Third Peer Conference:

How do you plan on incorporating these suggestions into your final monologue performance?

1. _____   _____

_____

_____

_____

2. _____   _____

_____

_____

_____

3. _____

_____

_____

_____

How did the costumes and props help in the creation of your character and the writing of your monologue? Be specific. (To be answered after you performed your monologue.)

_____

_____

_____

_____

_____

Questions to Think About
When Watching a Storytelling Video

1. How did the actor distinguish between the characters? Be specific.

_____

_____

_____

_____

2. What does he or she add to the stories (as a professional actor) that make them interesting?

_____

_____

_____

_____

3. How does the set add to the storytelling experiences?

_____

_____

_____

_____

4. How do the costumes and props add to the storytelling experience?

_____

_____

_____

_____

5. List the title of the story and its theme or moral.

_____

_____

_____

_____

6. What have you learned from watching this tape that will help you as a storyteller?

_____

_____

_____

_____

_____

_____

_____

_____

_____

_____

_____

_____

_____

Grade Assessment Sheets

RADIO SOUND EFFECTS PROJECT ASSESSMENT

Name _____

Objectives
- To create an exciting, imaginative radio drama from the play script given to your group.
- To add twenty-five different sound effects to the radio drama to enhance the story.

Process
- Daily cooperation
- Class goals met
- Deadlines met

Product
- Adaptation of script to radio play
- Use of sound effects to enhance story
- Projection and enunciation
- Overall dramatic effectiveness
- Technical considerations

Comments: _____
_____
_____
_____
_____
_____
_____
_____
_____
_____
_____

Group grade _____

Individual grade _____

STORYTELLING ASSESSMENT
SUPERHERO STORY

Name _____

Title of the story _____

Objectives
- To write an imaginative story with *you* as the main character. The story should have a clear story line and a beginning, middle, and end.
- To tell the story using all the skills and techniques that a professional storyteller would use.

1. Clarity of story line _____ _____

2. Use of voice _____

3. Facial expression _____

4. Energy and vitality _____

5. Focus and concentration_____

Comments: _____

_____
_____
_____
_____
_____
_____
_____
_____
_____

Grade _____

READERS THEATER WITH HATS
ASSESSMENT SHEET

Name _____

Production _____

Vocal expressiveness:

_____
_____

Facial expression:

_____
_____

Energy and vitality of performance:

_____
_____
_____

Characterization:

_____
_____
_____

Focus and concentration:

_____
_____

Familiarity with the script in the final performance:

_____
_____

Group grade _____
Individual grade _____

SPEECH ASSESSMENT:
Minispeeches/Speech to Persuade/
Time Machine Speech

Name _____

1. Organized speech?

2. Eye contact?

3. Energy?

4. Enunciation?

5. Projection?

6. Well-rehearscd?

7. Delivery?

8. Did the speech achieve its purpose?

9. Did you cover all the requirements?

Comments: _____

_____

_____

_____

_____

_____

_____

_____

_____

_____

_____

Minispeech grade   _____

Specch to persuade grade   _____

Time machine speech grade _____

GARAGE SALE MONOLOGUE ASSESSMENT

Name _____

1. Use of costumes and props

2. Is the monologue organized clearly?

3. Are the character's objectives clear?

4. Dramatic delivery

5. Memorization

Comments:_____
_____
_____
_____
_____
_____
_____
_____

Grade _____

GROUP EVALUATION
This form can be used for Paper Bag Players

On a scale of 0 percent to 100 percent, give each member of your group a grade in all of the listed areas below. List the members of the group below and then refer to them by their numbers in the rest of the evaluation.

1.

2.

3.

4.

Did the student contribute significantly to the creation of the play?

1.

2.

3.

4.

Did the student distract the group?

1.

2.

3.

4.

Did the student stay focused most of the time?

1.

2.

3.

4.

Were the student's ideas creative and original?

1.

2.

3.

4.

Did the student compromise easily when their ideas
were not accepted?

1.

2.

3.

4.

Did the student offer to do extra work (i.e., writing up the
script; bringing in props and costumes)

1.

2.

3.

4.

Was the student polite and attentive as an audience member?

1.

2.

3.

4.

Did the student concentrate when he or she was performing?

1.

2.

3.

4.

Did the group meet all the deadlines?

1.

2.

3.

4.

Was the final performance what you expected?

1.

2.

3.

4.

Please use the space below to add any written comments that you feel pertain to any group member's participation in this project. Feel free to evaluate your own contributions, too.

ASSESSMENT FOR PLAY PRODUCTION

Name _____

The assessment for play production is split into two sections: Process and Performance. You will receive a rating of Fair, Satisfactory, or Excellent for each category listed under Process and Performance. Specific comments on the entire experience of play production will be written at the end.

PROCESS

This section evaluates your day-to-day efforts during play production, from the first read-through to the dress rehearsal.

THE READ-THROUGH
Pronunciation/characterization
Attention to script reading
Willingness to read a part

TRYOUTS
Willingness to take risks during tryouts
Ability to take direction
Attitude toward role received

BLOCKING REHEARSALS
Prepared for rehearsal
Productive use of time (onstage and off)
Listening
Implementing (making the blocking look natural)
Line memorization
Community building attitude
Willingness to do extra work (i.e., stage prep, running lines)
Projection
Enunciation
Character formation (bringing the character to life)
Consistency of performance from class to class

PERFORMANCE

This section evaluates your performance in the final production of the play.

Deadlines met
Line memorization
Blocking memorization
Projection
Enunciation
Ease of movement onstage
Believable characterization
Sense of timing
Use of props
Growth as a performer

SPECIFIC COMMENTS

_____
_____
_____
_____
_____
_____
_____
_____
_____
_____
_____
_____
_____
_____
_____
_____

Grade _____

TIME OUT FOR DRAMA REFLECTION

Name _____

1. Has your group constructed or performed a clear,
    explanatory play? Give a short summary of how you
    arrived at the final production.

    _____

    _____

    _____

    _____

2. Comment on each person's cooperative attitude and give
    him or her the grade you think that he or she deserves.

Name _____ Grade _____

    _____

    _____

    _____

Name _____ Grade _____

    _____

    _____

    _____

Name _____ Grade _____

    _____

    _____

    _____

3. Do the same evaluation for yourself: Did you present
    solutions instead of roadblocks? Did you compromise?
    Did you meet all the deadlines?

    _____

    _____

    _____

    _____

Afterword

After *Middle Mania!* was published in February 2002, I heard from many teachers who found the book to be a valuable resource for teaching drama.

Tami Clancy wrote:

> I teach middle school drama to 8th, 7th, and 6th grade every day! Approximately 600 students rotate through my curriculum each year. The activities presented in *Middle Mania!* have prompted me to revamp my whole approach in teaching drama. They are fun, creative, easy to do, and feel a lot less stressful than continually preparing for large-scale productions.

A friend who teaches theater in Florida let a colleague look at her copy of the book and hasn't seen it since. Another friend checked *Middle Mania!* out of the library, read it, and went out and bought a copy for herself.

Linda Behen wrote in a review from *The Book Report*:

> Almost as soon as I began reading Johnson's book, I was thinking of individuals in our school with whom I could share it. Although it is written for theater teachers, it's useful for any teacher or administrator that might occasionally need an activity for community building. . . . Every school should have at least one copy.

Sue Krumbein writes in the *Voice of Youth Advocates:*

One of the many strengths of the book is its thoroughness. A teacher could offer an activity using this book and feel very comfortable about all the steps. Even the forms needed to assign, assess, and reflect are included at the end of the book. Frankly, the best feature of the book is that the reader feels as if he or she is having a conversation with the author, someone a teacher would very much like to meet.

I know that *Middle Mania Two!* will be the same kind of book — usable and teacher-friendly.

In *Middle Mania!* I wrote that "A drama-healthy curriculum provides every student with a chance to get involved. It gives the shy student a chance to build self-confidence. It also challenges boisterous students and stretches their imaginations."

These books represent more than a series of imaginative projects, though. They embody a philosophy of teaching that develops specific dramatic skills that build slowly upon each other, keeping even the shyest student safe onstage. The curriculum I developed for middle school is based on building community. The projects appeal to teachers of all disciplines because they connect naturally to those disciplines.

Since *Middle Mania!* was published, teachers from around the country and the world have written to me to express their relief at finding such a resource. I am thrilled to have written these books, books that are passed around from teacher to teacher and end up dog-eared with use.

My family and friends have asked me why it is so important to get up at 5:00 A.M. every day during vacation and work for six hours writing *Middle Mania Two!* I really believe that what I have discovered about teaching drama is not new. I just believe that it is important to tell my story.

Maureen Brady Johnson

Reflections on
Middle Mania! Projects

Chapter One: Radio Sound Effects Theater

Most youngsters today use their sight as a source of artistic inspiration. Using old radio shows helps young artists sharpen their imagination using senses other than the visual. In a radio broadcast the performers rely on sound effects, music and narration as well as dialogue to set the scene and portray the actions of the story. In essence, the music sets an emotional mood. The sound effects and narration set up the environment, and the dialogue carries the story line. These elements spark a visual impression of what you are hearing and this visual is different from person to person. This project gives the students a chance to concentrate on the use of their voice to carry their emotions and to include other elements to create and enhance the mood.

— Mark, parent and visual arts teacher

I liked trying to figure out which sounds to use. We used the stage door to make the sound of a door slamming. It was hard to get the timing right but it all turned out OK. The most fun we had was trying to come up with noises for the part when the people got stuck to the goose. We did all kinds of things with slurping noises. We laughed a lot so we had to rewind the tape and do it over again.

— David, student participant

Chapter Two: Storytelling

When we watched the videos on storytelling, they showed that there were many different dramatic possibilities when you told a story. The storytellers used their entire bodies to tell their stories. Jim Henson's "Storyteller" series showed us something different. It showed us how we could use sets, costumes and lighting to add to a story. We knew, though, that even if all those special effects were taken away, he could still tell a really good story.

— A. Marie, student participant

Every story has a beginning, a middle and an end. Mrs. J told us to pay attention to that and it really made a difference.

— Megan, student participant

Chapter Three: Readers Theater with Hats

I teach Eighth Grade social studies at Lake Ridge Academy and have no background in drama. One year the head of the Middle School needed someone to teach a drama option for a special offering in the fine arts that is done each spring. I agreed to teach it with one of my colleagues, the science teacher, if we could find something that was easy for us to do but worthwhile for the kids. We turned to Maureen Johnson, who provided us with a project that used various hats. The concept was simple, students loved it, and in about five weeks we were able to put on a performance in front of the middle school. The best part is that all of the creativity involved in the project came from the students who first developed characters, and then a play, with their hat as the inspiration.

— Mike Shaulis, social studies teacher

Chapter Four: Time Machine Speech

I remember introducing John Jones in the sixth grade as a cutting-edge aerospace engineer. I believe that he might have been working as the chief engineer in the company that I owned. But that's the sort of thing, I think, that makes the exercise a lot of fun.

— Jon, student participant

Our school had a young Russian exchange student in Middle School. Maria was painfully shy and rarely smiled. She was not making friends easily and language was a big barrier. I partnered her with a sensitive youngster and hoped for the best. When it came time for her introduction, she marched to the front of the room and had her partner hold up a stack of signs. The drawings on the signs were delightful cartoons and as she introduced her partner, she used the signs to illustrate her speech. When she was finished every student in the room applauded and after class, asked to see her drawings. Maria was so proud of herself. She smiled a lot after that day and had a minor role in the eighth grade play later that year!

— Mrs. Johnson

Chapter Five: Garage Sale Monologue

It was so much fun picking out something outrageous, like these shoes that I would *never* wear and then getting to write about a character who *would* wear those shoes. Putting them on and wearing them when I performed the monologue was a lot of fun, too.

— Allison, student participant

"Goodwill" Hunting

The characters really came alive for each of the children when we took a field trip to the Goodwill store. Each student was given a fixed amount they could spend on accessories to bring their character to life. It was this concrete experience that genuinely helped define the image created their imagination. What a powerful activity this was!

— Veronica Riffle, science teacher

Chapter Six: Paper Bag Players

Paper bag players is the ultimate group improv skit. It's a fun way to act crazy and to use props in unthinkable ways. One of my favorite paper bag items is a feather boa because it can be used to spice up any character. I remember one group doing a paper bag players skit that involved an eccentric talk show host and "extreme" guests, acting as outrageous as possible. Everyone had their props onstage, most of them being used in unconventional ways.

Paper bag players "saved" Student Council one year because is was raining on the day of our outdoor picnic/game day. We all gathered in the auditorium as all the organized teams (that were supposed to be outside!) and took turns creating crazy skits. It helped the time pass and our stomachs hurt afterwards because we had laughed so hard!

— Julia, student participant

Every year our Upper School starts the year with a day of fun, competitive games with teams made up of students from all four grades. As all the games take place outdoors, good weather is essential for this day's success. One year, rain interrupted our day of fun, forcing the entire Upper School into the auditorium. Maureen's Paper Bag Players exercise saved the day. Each team received a grocery bag of props and was told to create a skit using the props — the students had a GREAT time with this and were both creative and hilarious. Without Maureen's magic paper bags, I don't know what we would have done.

— Rachelle Bilz, student council sponsor

Chapter Seven: "Simple" Play Production

We had looked forward to the first quarter of eighth grade drama for a long time. Each class of approximately eighteen students performed a one-act play. Everything we had done previously was during the day and for our classmates, but the eighth grade play was at night, after school had let out. Our parents and friends came to watch us. We were big time actors on a stage with lights! During our sixteen week rehearsal period my classmates and I bonded on a new level. We leaned on each other for support as we tried to remember blocking and lines, weaning ourselves off our scripts. We knew that for an optimal performance we would have to completely trust our fellow actors. On performance night the princesses missed their cue and one of the princes had to improvise until they all got into their places. I will never forget the look on his face as he saw the empty space where the princesses were supposed to be! Since we had rehearsed for such a long time and trusted each other, the play continued with a few improvised lines and few audience members realized the mistake.

— J. Bilz, student participant

Eighth Grade Play

The costumes were so beautiful. They made me feel special because they were made especially for me! I wanted to do the best job I could, so I tried real hard to act my part. The costumes made me feel more confident onstage because I felt comfortable.

— Juliet, student participant

Eighth Grade plays . . . from a parent's point of view

Joyce offered to make costumes for a series of fairy-tale plays that we performed. They were exquisite medieval costumes made to fit students from middle school to upper school. We have used these adaptable costumes for years now. The students look like a million bucks onstage when they wear these gorgeous costumes. I asked her to sum up her years as a volunteer costumer and parent helper.

Find your imagination and allow it to create dreams! One of the greatest memories of my life are the fairy-tale plays I shared with my children and their friends. Pitch in, roll up your sleeves and get busy — there's room for everyone. You won't regret it!

— Joyce Money, parent volunteer

Why Teach Drama in Middle School?

Theater in Middle School not only encouraged me to be creative but also enabled me to have faith in my creativity. In drama class, I found a stage where I could let my imagination run wild and I always found the results rewarding. Whether it was a unit on storytelling, a monologue inspired by "junk," Clan Drama or the Mask/Movement project, I was always allowed to find my own creative voice.

In college, the strength I gained in middle school drama has proved invaluable, not just on the stage, but even in a purely academic environment. I see brilliant students cowering in discussion groups and staying away from lectures just because they are afraid to ask questions. Thanks to the influence of Mrs. J and her theater classes throughout my Middle and High School career, I am not one of the timid.

— Lakshman, Wooster College

Play Production in Middle School

"Treat each performer, no matter what age with respect. Let them know that theater is a collaborative effort. Encourage exploration. I always like trying all ideas (even those I'm sure to ultimately reject) for the first few rehearsals so that all involved will not be afraid to offer suggestions. Sometimes, even the most ridiculous idea can lead to something productive.

We always work on the back-story of each character. When there is a rehearsal that finishes a bit early, I use the time to explore characterization. The "trees" as well as the "stars" get a chance to tell the cast about who they are and each person's importance is clearly recognized.

Be clear about expectations. We did a production of *The Lion, The Witch and The Wardrobe* several years back. During the big battle scene where the Lion fights for the forces of good, there was no lion onstage. The actress was having a grand old time socializing backstage waiting for someone to fetch her. The actress didn't know that she was responsible for her own entrance.

We sometimes have a Middle School dance after the play. I love that. We have had great success with attendance and the performers get immediate feedback. I have also had great success with a kiddie matinee where we would invite the local preschools to an afternoon rehearsal. Great PR and if you have a quick "meet the cast" talk-back for the little ones, your own students are very gratified.

— Teresa Vigneaux, Head of Theater Department
St. Andrews School, Florida

It is all about respect.
- Respecting the audience by producing intelligent literature that does not pander to or insult a young spectator.
- Respecting the young artist by encouraging and supporting their artistic risks.
- Respecting the gift of experience that can only be passed on to the emerging artist from the adult professional artist by forming a bond of trust through the process of theatrical creation. And finally,
- Respecting the craft itself by keeping an open mind to every possibility.

— Katy Realista, playwright, director, teacher, www.Realistatheatre.com

Acting onstage is a paradox — everything matters but nothing matters. Every part is important. Every syllable has to be heard. Every gesture either contributes or detracts from the whole. On the other hand, if a student forgets a line or trips or falls — forget about it. It doesn't matter. If a student can embrace both of these simultaneously, you've got it.

Rather than focus on every nuance of character I wish my students would work on putting tension in their gestures, taking a beat after a funny bit or punching the last word with a "look." Energy and precision = Magic!

— Teresa Lee Jenkins, playwright, actress, teacher

Reviews from Teachers Who Use *Middle Mania!*

I love *Middle Mania!* Last September, when I was planning my curriculum for the upcoming school year, I really wanted to include a unit on drama for my fifth graders. I decided to use Maureen's unit on the Bag of Puppets — it was great! Maureen explains step-by-step what you need to do every day — from materials to worksheets and evaluations! For a busy teacher, this book is a godsend! I can't wait to do the Clan Drama unit second semester!
— Maureen Arbeznik, St. Luke School

Lately, my classes are just great! Today I witnessed my eighth graders busily working on their Rock-n-Roll project. One group even had a script ready and I must say it was really good — lots of potential. The important thing is that your book has definitely been a wonderful addition to my repertoire of lessons this year! My present class of eighth graders are having fun with this project and some are even requesting to perform it on the stage!!!!

Ideas are abundant with this new group. Today I had them plan, chat, and improvise. I had to encourage them to get up and try out some ideas. The group with the script made copies for everyone in their group and they were quite motivated to rehearse. They rehearsed quite independently and even started to choreograph their song. The last twenty-five minutes of today's class was devoted to sharing what they had accomplished today. They could share whatever they wanted to share. They rose to the occasion. They were amazed at the group's work with the completed script. Actually, that group was able to read the whole script and they did a fine job for a first run-through in front of an audience. The class loved it!

The important thing is that the kids are having a good time and I think we may have a few budding playwrights coming up. I find this so exciting!

This was the group that kept on planning and discussing their ideas after class was over.

I just thought that you would like to hear how the ideas from your book are working. Your book has been most instrumental in my reaching the present level of success in my middle school drama program! Thank you for your patience, assistance, guidance, inspiration and above all friendship.

After reading your book, I felt that I had just what I needed to be equipped and psyched to teach middle school drama. Having not taught drama for six years, your book gave me material I could use to inspire my students. The lessons and activities were well laid out and easy to follow.
— Barb Friedman, The American School of Warsaw, Warsaw, Poland